LECTURE READY

Strategies for Academic Listening, Note-taking, and Discussion

Peg Sarosy
American Language Institute
San Francisco State University

Kathy Sherak
American Language Institute
San Francisco State University

OXFORD
UNIVERSITY PRESS

OXFORD
UNIVERSITY PRESS

198 Madison Avenue
New York, NY 10016 USA

Great Clarendon Street
Oxford OX2 6DP UK

Oxford University Press is a department of the University of Oxford.
It furthers the University's objective of excellence in research, scholarship,
and education by publishing worldwide in

Oxford New York

Auckland Cape Town Dar es Salaam Hong Kong Karachi
Kuala Lumpu r Madrid Melbourne Mexico City Nairobi
New Delhi Shanghai Taipei Toronto

With offices in

Argentina Austria Brazil Chile Czech Republic France Greece
Guatemala Hungary Italy Japan Poland Portugal Singapore
South Korea Switzerland Thailand Turkey Ukraine Vietnam

OXFORD and OXFORD ENGLISH are registered trademarks of
Oxford University Press

© Oxford University Press 2006

Database right Oxford University Press (maker)

Executive Publisher: Janet Aitchison
Senior Acquisitions Editor: Pietro Alongi
Editor: Dena Daniel
Associate Editor: Martha Bordman
Art Director: Maj-Britt Hagsted
Design Project Manager: Nicoletta Barolini
Cover Design and Interior Lay-out: Delgado and Company
Art Editor: Justine Eun
Production Manager: Shanta Persaud
Production Controller: Eve Wong

Student Book
ISBN-13: 978 0 19 430968 4

Student Book pack (U.S. sales only)
ISBN-13: 978 0 19 441708 2

Printed in China

10 9 8 7 6 5 4 3

This book is printed on paper from certified and well-managed sources.

ACKNOWLEDGMENTS

Illustrations: Kenneth Batelman

We would like to thank the following for their permission to reproduce photographs:

Alamy: David Hoffman Photo Library, 56; Janine Wiedel Photolibrary, 54;
Dennis MacDonald, 98; Bill Varie, 24; Bruce Coleman, Inc: Jorge Calvo, 12;
The New Yorker Collection 1997 Leo Cullum from cartoonbank.com. All
Rights Reserved, 90; Justine Eun for OUP: 68, 82; Randy Glasbergen: 46;
Omni-Photo Communications: Tom Stillo, 108; PhotoEdit: David Young-
Wolff, 2; Punchstock: Bananastock, 25, 64, 76, 78, 86; CORBIS: 57;
Photodisc, 10, 42; Purestock, 91; USDA and DHHS: 47.

We also would like to thank the following for their help:

"American Time Use Survey," 2003. Bureau of Labor Statistics web site
(www.bls.gov).

"Children and Ozone Air Pollution Fact Sheet," Information reprinted
with permission © 2005 American Lung Association. For more
information about the American Lung Association or to support the work
it does, call 1-800-LUNG-USA (1-800-586-4872) or log on to
www.lungusa.org.

"Fact Sheet: Respiratory Health Effects of Passive Smoking," 1993. U.S.
Environmental Protection Agency web site (www.epa.gov).

Media Literacy by James Potter, 2000. Information used by permission of
Sage Publications Inc.

News in a New Century by Jerry Lanson and Barbara Croll Fought, 1999.
Information used by permission of Sage Publications Inc.

Teenage dialogue by Dominique Ameroso and Olivia Karwowski, 2005.

Introduction

Lecture Ready: Strategies for Academic Listening, Note-taking, and Discussion trains students for academic success. *Lecture Ready 2* is intended for students at the intermediate level. Students learn how to listen to lectures and take notes effectively, and to communicate with other students in group discussions. Through the use of engaging lectures presented via DVD, students experience the demands and atmosphere of a real college classroom. This preparation enables students to enter a college or university armed with the strategies they need to listen, take notes, and discuss ideas independently and confidently.

Thoroughly Integrated Academic Listening and Speaking

In college and university settings, students not only listen to lectures but also discuss the ideas in the lecture with classmates and the instructor, drawing on the knowledge gained through listening. By integrating academic listening and speaking, this book enriches the training for academic readiness. Students also learn key vocabulary selected from the **Academic Word List**, orginally developed by Averil Coxhead.* Vocabulary is first presented in context in a reading passage then practiced throughout the listening and speaking process.

A Focus on Strategies

In order to become proficient listeners and speakers, students need strategies that will help them meet their listening and speaking challenges in and beyond the language classroom. Listening to isolated listening exercises provides only limited instruction; students need to learn a process for each stage of listening. Similarly, rather than simply speaking and being evaluated in response to a question, students need to learn the language and strategies for successfully engaging in classroom discussions—strategies that they can apply throughout their academic career.

In *Lecture Ready*, students learn and practice a variety of listening, note-taking, and discussion strategies before they watch an actual lecture and participate in an extended class discussion about the ideas in the lecture.

Students learn two types of listening strategies:

- strategies for independently preparing for each stage of the listening process—before a lecture, during a lecture, and after a lecture
- strategies for recognizing "lecture language" — the discourse markers, speech features, and lexical bundles that lecturers across disciplines commonly use to guide students in taking in information

Note-taking strategies focus the students' attention on the accurate and concise recording of material delivered during a lecture. They learn that effective note-taking is the cornerstone of effective studying.

Students also learn discussion strategies. These strategies clue students in to university classroom expectations for participation. They also allow students to practice the language necessary for becoming an active member of a classroom discussion.

Academic Readiness

Lecture Ready prepares students for the challenges of academic work by training them in effective study habits. Each chapter focuses on strategies that maximize student achievement at each stage of the lesson.

Students prepare for a lecture by reading something on a relevant topic in one of a variety of formats. The readings introduce vocabulary important for students' understanding of the main lecture material.

Before watching the lecture, students review what they already know on the topic and make predictions. During the lecture, students listen actively and take notes (aided by a structure in the earlier chapters, unaided in the later chapters). After the lecture, students solidify their understanding by using their notes to review and summarize the lecture.

The last step is discussion. Students participate in small group discussions, drawing on the information presented in the lecture.

Visual Listening Materials: Lectures on DVD

During an academic lecture, listeners comprehend by making sense of what they hear *and* what they see. Visual cues such as gestures, movement, and board work are an integral part of the spoken message. Without these visual cues, effective listening is challenging for even the most accomplished student. *Lecture Ready* allows students to fully engage in the lecture experience by watching each chapter's centerpiece lecture on DVD.

The lectures present facts and research findings as well as their implications. The lectures also feature all the characteristics of true academic lectures: natural language, pauses, backtracking, false starts, recapping, filler words, stalling, and other hallmarks of one-way communication. All lectures feature the "lecture language" presented and practiced in each chapter.

Engaging Content

In *Lecture Ready*, students learn about and discuss content from a variety of academic fields—topics that speak to the world they live in. The ten centerpiece lectures contain the type of material found in introductory university courses in five academic content areas: business and marketing, sociology, science, media studies, and linguistics. Chapter topics are designed to appeal to a wide range of student backgrounds and are conducive to class discussions that draw on multiple perspectives.

Positive Results

Students are more competent and confident when they learn *how to listen* and *how to discuss ideas* using proven strategies for academic success. With *Lecture Ready*, students learn these strategies explicitly, helping them understand and adopt effective techniques for academic progress. Students also gain a familiarity with the vocabulary, lecture language, and atmosphere of a real classroom. *Lecture Ready: Strategies for Academic Listening, Note-taking, and Discussion* enables students to make the transition from textbook lessons to successful encounters with real life academic lectures and discussions.

Organization of the Book

Lecture Ready 2: Strategies for Academic Listening, Note-taking, and Discussion contains five units with two chapters in each unit. Each unit focuses on one field of academic study. Each chapter is built around a lecture from a typical course within the field. In each chapter, students are presented with and practice listening, note-taking, and discussion strategies.

Chapters consist of the following components:

- **Build Background Knowledge**
  Think about the topic, reading passage, vocabulary work, review

- **Prepare to Listen and Take Notes**
  Listening strategy, lecture language, practice lecture (listening strategy practice), note-taking strategy, note-taking strategy practice

- **Listen and Take Notes**
  Predictions, lecture, comprehension, summarizing

- **Discuss the Issues**
  Discussion strategy, strategy practice, discussion

Acknowledgements

We'd like to express our gratitude to the following people who played a role in the creation of this book:

Dr. H. Douglas Brown, Director of the American Language Institute, who has inspired us through his own work with strategy-based instruction and who has given us the encouragement and freedom to continue to develop our professional selves.

The many professors at San Francisco State University who generously opened their doors to allow us to attend their classes and listen for all the real life examples of engaging lectures rich with lecture language.

Dr. David Mendelsohn, who inspired us to take up the challenge of teaching listening with a strategy-based approach.

Nicole Frantz, Mary Lou King, and Sandra Osumi, our colleagues at the ALI, for their interest and support all through the process.

The teachers at the ALI, for being open to new ideas, which in turn has inspired us to see the possibilities and push the pedagogical envelope.

ALI students and teachers for their help with piloting lectures and materials.

Moya Brennan, Darlene Elwin, Marcella Farina, Pat Ishill, Barbara Mattingly, Carla Nyssen, Adrianne Ochoa, and especially Gretchen Owens for reviewing lecture content.

The editorial team at Oxford University Press, Janet Aitchison, Pietro Alongi, and Dena Daniel, for their vision, encouragement, and guidance.

Finally, to our families, Christine, Maggie, Chaen, and Gabriel, for saying yes… again and again.

Lecture Ready Program

The *Lecture Ready* program consists of three components:

Student book

contains the readings, strategy explanations, and exercises for the *Lecture Ready* program.

Audio program

(CDs or cassettes) contains the audio-only targeted lecture language exercises necessary to each chapter. These exercises are marked with the audio icon.

Video program

(DVD or VHS) contains the centerpiece lectures for each chapter and the lecture language exercise for Chapter 8 (visual cues). These exercises are marked with the video icon.

Contents

Listening Strategies	Note-taking Strategies	Discussion Strategies
Recognize lecture language that signals the topic and big picture of a lecture	Write down key words and ideas from the lecture in your notes	Enter a discussion about the ideas in a lecture
Recognize other lecture language that signals the big picture of a lecture	Use an informal outline to take notes Use your notes to give a spoken summary of a lecture	Contribute your ideas in a discussion
Recognize lecture language that signals a transition between ideas in a lecture	Use symbols to represent words and ideas in your notes	Interrupt and ask for clarification during a discussion
Recognize lecture language that signals a definition	Use abbreviations to represent words and ideas in your notes	Ask for more information during a discussion
Recognize lecture language that signals an example	Organize key lecture material in visual form in your notes	Agree and disagree during a discussion
Recognize lecture language that signals an explanation	Describe the graphics used in a lecture in your notes	Support your opinions during a discussion
Recognize lecture language that signals when information is important	Highlight key ideas in your notes	Connect your ideas to other people's ideas in a discussion
Recognize non-verbal signals that indicate when information is important	Annotate your notes	Keep the discussion focused on the topic
Recognize changes in pronunciation that signal when information is important	Edit your notes	Encourage other students to participate during a discussion
Review and practice all listening strategies	Review and practice all note-taking strategies	Bring a group to a consensus during a discussion

Contents

To the Student

If you are planning to enter college or university for the first time, you face two equally big challenges: how to understand all of the complex content in academic lectures, and how to communicate effectively with classmates and professors.

Lecture Ready 2: Strategies for Academic Listening, Note-taking, and Discussion will help you face these challenges by giving you the strategies you need for success in your academic career. You will learn to do all the things that successful students do—listen actively to lectures, take effective notes, and participate confidently in discussions about the lecture with classmates. While learning these strategies, you will also learn and use common academic vocabulary as well as useful idioms.

Lecture Ready presents lively and interesting lectures on DVD. These lectures are on a variety of topics from many different fields of study. The lectures were created to be just like the lectures that students encounter in a college or university.

What You Will Learn

The **listening strategies** in *Lecture Ready* prepare you for each stage of the listening process. You will learn how to use the knowledge that you already have to prepare to take in new information. You will become familiar with lecture language, which will help you follow the ideas during a lecture. You will learn how to bring together all the information from a lecture so that you can better understand, remember, and use what you have learned. Listening strategies help you get the most out of a lecture.

The **note-taking strategies** focus on the way information can be represented on paper. You will learn about and practice useful methods for taking effective notes during a lecture class. You can practice your new note-taking skills during the lecture, too.

The **discussion strategies** are meant to help you feel comfortable discussing information from the lecture with classmates. Many students feel uncertain about taking part in class discussions because they are not sure what to say, when to say it, or how to say it. With *Lecture Ready*, you can learn what professors expect from you and what you should deliver in return. You will learn specific strategies to make you a more confident speaker no matter what subject you are discussing.

Have fun, and enjoy the academic experiences, challenges, and strategies that *Lecture Ready* has to offer.

unit
1

MARKETING

marketing \\'mɑrkəʈɪŋ\\ The study of the processes and techniques involved with promoting, selling, and distributing a product or service

Chapter 1 | Gender and Spending

CHAPTER GOALS

- Learn about differences in how men and women spend money and how this affects marketing
- Learn a Listening Strategy: Recognize lecture language that signals the topic and big picture of a lecture
- Learn a Note-taking Strategy: Write down the key words and ideas in a lecture
- Learn a Discussion Strategy: Enter a discussion about the ideas in a lecture

Build Background Knowledge

Think about the topic

1. Look at the picture of a man and woman shopping together. Then do the exercise below in pairs.

Imagine this situation. A man and woman go together to a big department store. The store has a wide variety of products—clothes, computers, food, appliances, automotive supplies, furniture. They decide to separate and meet again in an hour.

1. What things will the man probably shop for?

2. What things will the woman probably shop for?

3. In the same situation, what would you probably shop for? Do you think you are typical or unusual? Why?

2. Read this article about the changing shopping habits of women.

WOMEN ENTER THE ELECTRONICS MARKET

Just as the roles and responsibilities of men and women are changing in society, so are the shopping habits of the two **genders**. The electronics industry (computers, cell phones, digital cameras, etc.) is one place where gender differences in purchasing are rapidly changing.

Until very recently, the electronics **market** consisted mostly of men. Today, however, women are some of the biggest **consumers** of computers and other electronic products. With more and more women working and in control of their own and their family's money, women now want to **have a say** in the type of electronics that they have in their homes. Some experts report that women are actually buying more electronics than men. A recent **study** by the Consumer Electronics Association reports another interesting development. It states that almost a third of the new and more **innovative** electronics are sold to women. So, not only are women becoming more interested in electronics purchases in general, but they are also increasingly willing to try the latest products.

Women in the U.S. are now spending more than $50 billion on electronics. What are the **implications** of this change in women's spending habits for marketing? Laura Heller, senior editor of *DSN Retailing Today*, believes that until recently women have been ignored by the electronics industry. She says, "There's so much we don't know about this group: How they shop for electronics, how

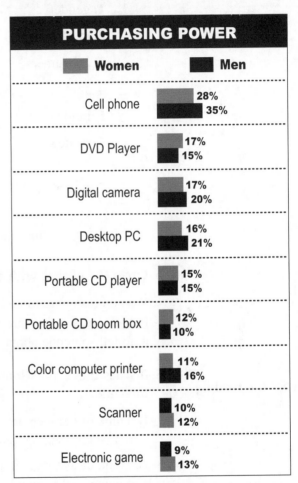

PURCHASING POWER

Women | Men

	Women	Men
Cell phone	28%	35%
DVD Player	17%	15%
Digital camera	17%	20%
Desktop PC	16%	21%
Portable CD player	15%	15%
Portable CD boom box	12%	10%
Color computer printer	11%	16%
Scanner	12%	10%
Electronic game	13%	9%

they feel about these products, and more importantly, how these products make them feel." Businesses need to understand the changes in their customer population and create new **strategies** to meet consumers' needs. These strategies will focus on the need to **appeal** to their new customers, that is, to appeal to women.

3. Answer the questions about the article on page 3. Then discuss your answers with a partner.

1. What is one change in the way that women spend money?

2. What's one interesting development in the electronics industry today?

3. What do electronics marketers want to find out about women?

4. Match the words with their definitions. Look back at the article on page 3 to check your answers.

_____ 1. gender

_____ 2. market

_____ 3. consumers

_____ 4. study

_____ 5. innovative

_____ 6. strategies

_____ 7. appeal

_____ 8. implications

a. people who buy things or use services

b. to be attractive or interesting to someone

c. developed using new ways of thinking

d. plans that are used to achieve a goal

e. a research project about a particular subject

f. classification of people into two sexes, male and female

g. the effects that something will have on something in the future

h. group of people who might buy a particular thing

5. Circle the phrase with a similar meaning to the underlined idiom.

Women today are more involved in family finances, so they also want to have a say in purchasing decisions for the home.

a. to tell someone about   **b.** to be part of   **c.** to make

6. Discuss these questions in a small group. Share your answers with the class.

1. Think of the men and women that you know. What changes have you noticed in their shopping interests? Give some examples.

2. Think of a store that usually appeals to men. What could it do to appeal to women? What could a "woman's" store do to appeal to men?

Review What You Know
To help you get ready to take in new information during the lecture, first think about what you already know about the topic.

Review what
you know

7. With a partner, write down three things that you have learned so far about gender and spending.

1. _____

2. _____

3. _____

Prepare to Listen and Take Notes

1. To help you understand the listening strategy, discuss the situation below and answer the questions.

You arrive five minutes late to class, and the professor has already begun. You start to take notes, but you are not sure what the lecture is about. Then, you notice that your classmates are following the lecture easily and taking organized notes. What information did you miss at the beginning of the lecture? Why is this information important?

Recognize Lecture Language for the Topic and Big Picture
At the beginning of a lecture, professors usually tell you the topic, or what the lecture is going to be about. They also give you the big picture—the general plan of the lecture. The big picture is an overview of how the professor will present the material, like a map of the lecture.

Listen for the words and expressions that professors use to indicate the topic. Also, listen for the words and expressions that professors use to indicate the big picture.

Listening Strategy

Topic lecture
language

2. Read the expressions that signal the topic of a lecture. Can you add others to the list?

Our topic today is . . .   _____
We'll be talking about . . .
What I want to talk about today is . . .   _____
We'll be discussing . . .
We're going to look at . . .   _____
Let's go back to our discussion of . . .
Let's continue our discussion of . . .

3. Read the expressions that signal the big picture of a lecture. Can you add others to the list?

First, we'll look at _____ and then we'll move on to look at _____
I'm going to cover _____ and then _____
We'll discuss several reasons for _____
I'm going to give you a few examples of/types of _____

_____

_____

_____

4. Read this lecture introduction. Circle the topic. Then underline and label the lecture language that signals the topic and the lecture language that signals the big picture.

Let's get started because the topic today is really interesting. What I want to talk about is how people spend money. This is a really popular topic because everyone has a personal story about spending money. Okay, so first we'll look at the spending habits of wealthy people and then we'll move on to the spending habits of the poor.

5. Listen to the introductions of three different lectures. First, listen to each introduction and write down the topic lecture language and the topic. Then listen to each introduction again and write down the big picture lecture language.

1. Topic lecture language: _____

Topic: _____

Big picture lecture language: _____

2. Topic lecture language: _____

Topic: _____

Big picture lecture language: _____

3. Topic lecture language: _____

Topic: _____

Big picture lecture language: _____

Write the Most Important Words
During a lecture, you do not have time to write down every word that a professor says. Write down the words that have the most meaning in the lecture.

Write the most
important words

6. Read the transcript from a lecture on how men spend money. Then, look at one student's notes from the lecture. Cross out the words in the lecture that are not in the notes. The first sentence has been done for you.

....

~~Our~~ topic ~~is~~ trends in gender ~~and~~ spending. New trends are in the electronics industry…. marketers and advertisers want to know the kinds of electronics women are buying and the electronic products men are buying.

....

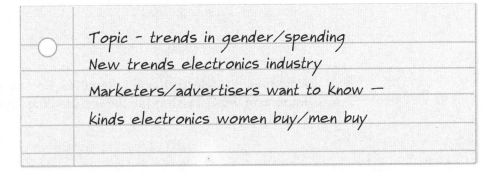

Topic - trends in gender/spending
New trends electronics industry
Marketers/advertisers want to know —
kinds electronics women buy/men buy

The words that are not important to the meaning of the professor's ideas are usually in these categories:

Pronouns: our, my, their, . . .   **Prepositions**: in, on, at, . . .
Helping verbs: be, have, do   **Conjunctions**: and, but, so, . . .
Determiners: a, the, this, . . .

7. Read these sentences from a lecture on trends in spending. Write down only the words that have the most meaning in the lecture.

1. In the past, the electronics market consisted mostly of men.

_____

2. Almost a third of the new and more innovative electronics are being sold to women.

_____

3. Businesses have only recently noticed the change in their customer base and are beginning to create new strategies to try to appeal to women.

_____

Listen and Take Notes

Predict
To help you get ready for new information and listen more actively, think about what the professor might discuss in the lecture. Make a prediction based on what you already know.

Make predictions

1. **Before the lecture, think about everything you have learned and discussed on the topic of gender and spending. What do you expect to learn more about in the lecture? Write three predictions below. Compare your predictions with a partner.**

   1. *I expect to learn more about ...* _____

   2. _____

   3. _____

Follow the lecture

2. **Now follow the lecture and take notes. Be sure to write down the most important words. Listen for the lecture language that signals the topic and big picture.**

Topic: _____

Ways men and women spend money and reactions by business _____

_____

Traditional responsibilities for women _____

_____

Traditional responsibilities for men _____

_____

Changes to traditional roles _____

_____

Changes in spending _____

_____

Meaning for business _____

_____

Marketing to women _____

_____

3. How well were you able to recognize the lecture language? Check the statement that best describes you. Explain your answer.

_____ I was able to recognize when the lecturer said the topic and big picture of the lecture.

_____ I didn't recognize when the lecturer said the topic and big picture of the lecture.

4. Use your notes to answer these questions.

1. Traditionally, what type of things were women responsible for buying?

_____

_____

2. Traditionally, what type of things were men responsible for buying?

_____

_____

3. What are the two reasons for the change in women's shopping habits?

_____

_____

4. What are three examples of ways that businesses are trying to become female friendly?

_____

_____

_____

Note-taking Strategy

Assess Your Notes
During a lecture, you can sometimes miss an important idea or piece of information. Compare notes with classmates in a study group after the lecture to check that your notes are complete.

5. Were you able to answer the questions in Exercise 4 using the information in your notes? Compare your notes with a few other students. Discuss the differences and help each other fill in any missing information—words, definitions, ideas. Complete your notes.

Discuss the Issues

Discussion Strategy

Enter the Discussion
You will often be asked to discuss the lecture's ideas with the whole class or with a small group of classmates. In these discussions, professors expect all students to participate actively. Do not wait for someone to ask you to speak. Instead, use expressions to get into the discussion so that you can contribute your ideas.

Enter the
discussion

1. Read the expressions for entering a discussion. Can you add any others to the list?

I'd like to say something here.	Can I add something to that?
I'd like to comment on that.	I have a question about that.
Can I say something here?	I'd like to add my two cents.

_____

_____

_____

Note: Speakers often say a small word or interjection to get attention before using one of the expressions above:

Well,... I'd like to say something here.
Yes,... I have a question about that.
So,... Can I say something here?
Um,... I'd like to add my two cents.

Practice entering the discussion

2. In groups of four, read the questions and discuss them. Keep the conversation going until every student has had the chance to practice entering the discussion. Use your own ideas or the ones given below.

1. Where do women like to shop?

Possible Ideas

Stores that:
  are small
  have clear signs
  have nice lighting
  have helpful clerks

2. Where do men like to shop?

Possible Ideas

Stores that:
  are on the Internet
  have a bigvariety of products
  have quick service
  have knowledgeable clerks

Discuss the ideas in the lecture

3. Discuss these ideas from the lecture with your classmates. Remember to use the phrases for entering the discussion.

1. The professor pointed out that more and more women are making "big ticket" purchases such as computers and cars. Do you think this is true? Have you seen evidence of this change in spending habits?

2. According to the lecture, marketers are now trying to appeal more to women. Do you think marketers need to use different marketing strategies for men and for women?

3. If you were a marketing manager, how would you increase the appeal of a computer store (or car repair shop or hardware store) to women? How would you increase the appeal of a home decoration store (or supermarket or day spa) to men?

4. Look back at your notes. What was another idea in the lecture that you found important and interesting? Tell the class why you think it is important or interesting and ask for their opinions.

apter 2 | Ads Are Everywhere

CHAPTER GOALS | • Learn about the reasons behind recent increases in advertising.
• Learn a Listening Strategy: Recognize other lecture language that signals the big picture of a lecture
• Learn a Note-taking Strategy: Use an informal outline
• Learn a Discussion Strategy: Contribute your ideas to a discussion

Build Background Knowledge

Think about the topic

1. Look at the picture. Then discuss the questions below in pairs.

1. How many advertisements do you think you see in a typical day? Trace your steps and list the places.

2. Do you think you see more ads now than you saw 10 years ago? Why or why not?

2. Students in a Principles of Marketing course had to write a report about all of the advertising they encountered in a single day. Read one student's online diary about his experiences with advertising while carrying out the assignment.

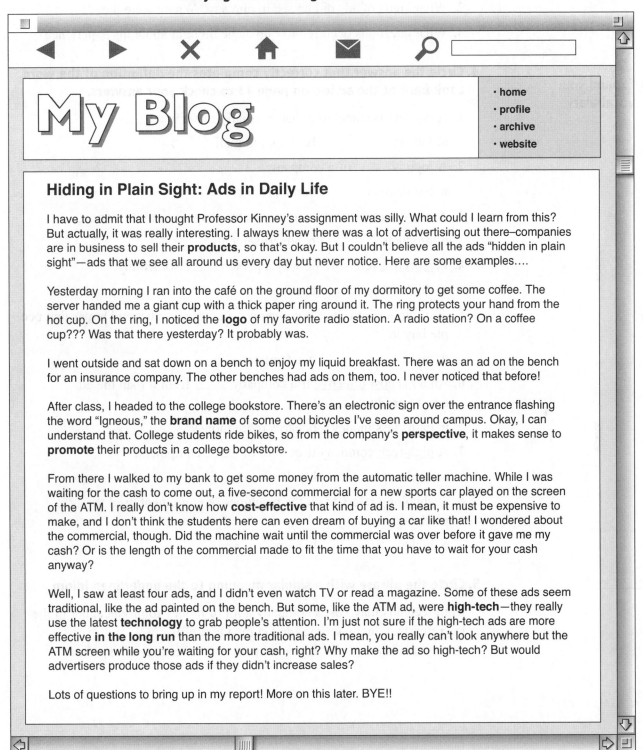

My Blog

- home
- profile
- archive
- website

Hiding in Plain Sight: Ads in Daily Life

I have to admit that I thought Professor Kinney's assignment was silly. What could I learn from this? But actually, it was really interesting. I always knew there was a lot of advertising out there–companies are in business to sell their **products**, so that's okay. But I couldn't believe all the ads "hidden in plain sight"—ads that we see all around us every day but never notice. Here are some examples….

Yesterday morning I ran into the café on the ground floor of my dormitory to get some coffee. The server handed me a giant cup with a thick paper ring around it. The ring protects your hand from the hot cup. On the ring, I noticed the **logo** of my favorite radio station. A radio station? On a coffee cup??? Was that there yesterday? It probably was.

I went outside and sat down on a bench to enjoy my liquid breakfast. There was an ad on the bench for an insurance company. The other benches had ads on them, too. I never noticed that before!

After class, I headed to the college bookstore. There's an electronic sign over the entrance flashing the word "Igneous," the **brand name** of some cool bicycles I've seen around campus. Okay, I can understand that. College students ride bikes, so from the company's **perspective**, it makes sense to **promote** their products in a college bookstore.

From there I walked to my bank to get some money from the automatic teller machine. While I was waiting for the cash to come out, a five-second commercial for a new sports car played on the screen of the ATM. I really don't know how **cost-effective** that kind of ad is. I mean, it must be expensive to make, and I don't think the students here can even dream of buying a car like that! I wondered about the commercial, though. Did the machine wait until the commercial was over before it gave me my cash? Or is the length of the commercial made to fit the time that you have to wait for your cash anyway?

Well, I saw at least four ads, and I didn't even watch TV or read a magazine. Some of these ads seem traditional, like the ad painted on the bench. But some, like the ATM ad, were **high-tech**—they really use the latest **technology** to grab people's attention. I'm just not sure if the high-tech ads are more effective **in the long run** than the more traditional ads. I mean, you really can't look anywhere but the ATM screen while you're waiting for your cash, right? Why make the ad so high-tech? But would advertisers produce those ads if they didn't increase sales?

Lots of questions to bring up in my report! More on this later. BYE!!

3. Answer the questions about the reading on page 13. Then discuss your answers with a partner.

1. What surprised the student about this assignment?

2. What kinds of ads did he see in one day? Where were they?

3. What questions occurred to him as he thought about his experience?

4. Circle the answer that correctly completes the definition of the word. Look back at the article on page 13 to check your answers.

1. A <u>product</u> is something that is usually made in a _____ .

   a. factory   **b.** shopping mall

2. A <u>logo</u> is _____ of a company.

   a. the symbol   **b.** the product

3. A <u>brand name</u> is the name that a company gives to its own _____ .

   a. products   **b.** advertisements

4. <u>Perspective</u> refers to the way a person _____ something.

   a. thinks about   **b.** earns

5. To <u>promote</u> a product, a company _____ the product and hopes that people buy it.

   a. makes   **b.** advertises

6. An ad is <u>cost-effective</u> if a company _____ from it than the ad cost to produce.

   a. earns less money   **b.** earns more money

7. A <u>high-tech</u> company uses a lot of _____ equipment.

   a. modern   **b.** tall

8. <u>Technology</u> refers to all the machines or equipment used to _____ products.

   a. make   **b.** name

5. Circle the phrase with a similar meaning to the underlined idiom.

High-tech ads may cost a company a lot of money to produce, but <u>in the long run</u>, they increase sales and company profits.

a. very quickly   **b.** sometimes   **c.** over a long time

6. Discuss these questions in a small group. Share your answers with the class.

1. Do you think the number and placement of the ads that the student saw is unusual? Why or why not? How do you feel about ads that are "hidden in plain sight"?

2. Why do you think advertisers use these kinds of ads?

7. With a partner, write down three things that you have learned so far about advertising.

1. _____

2. _____

3. _____

Prepare to Listen and Take Notes

Recognize Lecture Language for the Big Picture

A professor can give you the big picture, or general plan, of a lecture in a variety of ways. Often a professor uses an expression that tells you specifically how he or she will present the material in the lecture.

Listen for the words and expressions that professors use to signal the big picture.

1. Read the expressions that signal the big picture of a lecture. Can you add others to the list?

Today, I'm going to look at two aspects of _____

Now, what I want to do is discuss the causes of _____

We'll look at several ways that _____

What I want to do today is compare _____ and _____

I want to give you some background on _____

_____

_____

_____

**2. Read each lecture introduction. Circle the topic. Then underline and
label the lecture language that signals the topic and the big picture.**

Lecture 1

Good afternoon. It's nice to see you all. It looks like you are ready to go, so let's get
started. We'll be talking about techniques that advertisers use to sell movies. So think
about the last movie that you saw. Got it? Do you remember what made you go see
the movie? OK. Well, this morning, we'll look at several ways that the movie industry
advertises to movie-goers.

Lecture 2

Hi everyone. Please take your seats so we can get started. Great. In today's lecture
we're going to look at how high-tech products are advertised. Now, to help understand
how sophisticated these ads are, I want to give you some background on the products
and the education level of the people who use them.

**3. Listen to the introductions of three different lectures. Listen for
the lecture language that signals the topic and write the topic of each
lecture below.**

1. Topic: _____

2. Topic: _____

3. Topic: _____

**4. Listen to the introductions again. For each introduction, write down
the big picture lecture language.**

1. Big picture lecture language: _____

_____

_____

2. Big picture lecture language: _____

_____

_____

3. Big picture lecture language: _____

_____

_____

Use an Informal Outline
Your notes should give you an accurate record of the ideas in the lecture and show you how different points are related to each other. Organizing your notes in an outline form—using indentation—helps you remember which information is most important and which information is related but less important, such as examples, definitions, and dates.

Take notes in outline form

5. Read the transcript from a lecture on how men spend money. Then, look at one student's notes from the lecture. Answer the questions below.

All right…Now I want to talk about the three ways that advertisers appeal to consumers. They use facts, statistics, and research reports. A typical example of a research report is the ad where you see the doctor who says that a pill will help decrease pain by 23%.

> 3 ways advertisers appeal to consumers
>   facts
>   statistics
>   research reports
>   typical example: doctor in ad says
>   pill decreases pain 23%

1. What is the topic in this part of the lecture? How does the student indicate this in his/her notes?

2. What are the three ways that advertisers appeal to people? How does the student indicate this?

3. Why is "typical example" indented under "research reports"?

6. Read this transcript from a lecture on advertising. Take notes in outline form in your notebook.

Let's move on to discuss emotional appeals in advertising. Emotional appeals are advertising messages that try to create a feeling about a product. So you might see an emotional appeal in an ad for a product that makes the person feel happy. A good example of this is the soft drink ad that shows people laughing and having a great time at a party… and we see someone at the party who is holding the soft drink. Another example of that is a car ad that shows a well-dressed person driving an expensive car through beautiful scenery. This makes you feel wealthy and powerful. With both of these ads you begin to have a good feeling about the product… and the advertisers think maybe you'll go out and buy that product.

Listen and Take Notes

Make predictions

▷ p. 8

1. **Before the lecture, think about everything you have learned and discussed on the topic of advertising. What do you expect to learn more about in the lecture? Write three predictions below. Compare your predictions with a partner.**

   1. _____

   2. _____

   3. _____

Follow the lecture

▷ outline, p. 17

2. **Now follow the lecture and take notes using an informal outline. Remember to listen for the lecture language that signals the big picture.**

Topic: _____

Reasons ads are everywhere _____

_____

_____

One new kind of advertising _____

_____

_____

Another new kind of advertising _____

_____

_____

From advertisers' perspective _____

_____

_____

Reasons for increase in advertising _____

_____

_____

Assess your comprehension

3. How well were you able to recognize the lecture language? Check the statement that best describes you. Explain your answer.

_____ I was able to recognize when the lecturer said the big picture of the lecture.

_____ I didn't recognize when the lecturer said the big picture of the lecture.

4. Use your notes to answer these questions.

1. What are the two new kinds of ads explained in the lecture? Give one example of each new kind of ad.

_____

_____

2. What are the advantages of "hidden" ads for advertisers?

_____

_____

3. What are some reasons for the increase in advertising?

_____

_____

4. What is an example of how technology has contributed to the rise in advertising?

_____

_____

_____

Note-taking Strategy

Summarize the Lecture
A good way to help remember a lecture is to put the key ideas into your own words. This will also help you confirm that you understood all the information and that your notes are complete.

As soon as possible after a lecture, put the key ideas into your own words and speak them out loud to a study partner or to yourself.

Summarize the lecture

Imagine this situation: Your friend had to miss class because he was ill. The next day, he asks you to tell him about the lecture. What would you tell him? You would probably give him the following information:

• the topic of the lecture

• the big picture of the lecture (the most important ideas)

• a few important points and examples

This is the same information that you use when you summarize.

5. Read these expressions for summarizing.

The professor talked about _____   And then he discussed _____
She explained. . .   He gave us the example of. . .
She told us. . .   After that he wrapped up with. . .
He said that. . .

6. Work with a partner and take turns. Summarize the lecture out loud. Explain the main points of the lecture to your partner. Talk for 2-3 minutes only.

Did you both understand all the points in the lecture? Did you both catch all the information?

Discuss the Issues

Discussion Strategy

Contribute to the Discussion
You can contribute your ideas throughout a discussion. Your ideas might be important or interesting points from the lecture, comments and observations about the topic, or your own opinions. Use expressions to show that you want to contribute something to the discussion.

1. Read the expressions for contributing to the discussion. Can you add others to the list?

I think it was interesting that . . .   I think/feel . . .
I noticed that . . .   In my opinion, . . .
I was wondering if . . .   To me, . . .
_____ is a good example of _____   _____ is really important/
                                            interesting because . . .

_____

_____

_____

Practice contributing to the discussion

2. In groups of four, read the questions and discuss them. Keep the conversation going until every student has had a chance to practice contributing to the discussion. Use your own ideas or the ones given below.

1. In a typical day, where do you see advertisements?

   Possible Ideas

on buses	on the grocery store floor
on the ATM machine	at sports stadiums
on park benches	on the Internet

2. What kinds of ads do you enjoy looking at—for which types of products? Why?

   Possible Ideas

health products	cell phones
sports equipment	drugs
cars	clothes
make up	computers

Discuss the ideas in the lecture

3. Discuss these ideas from the lecture with your classmates. Remember to use the phrases for contributing ideas to the discussion.

1. The professor talked about ads that don't seem like ads. What other examples of this kind of advertising have you seen? Why do companies use "hidden ads"? How do you feel about them?

2. In the United States, there are restrictions on the placement of certain types of advertising. For example, there on no ads for cigarettes on television to help discourage smoking. Is it fair that the advertising for some products is restricted? Why or why not? What types of products probably have restrictions on their advertising? Why?

3. Imagine that your company wants to advertise at a baseball stadium. You can choose to have a painted sign on the back fence or an electronic ad that will appear only on television. Which type of ad would you suggest? Why?

4. Look back at your notes. What was another idea in the lecture that you found important and interesting? Tell the class why you think it is important or interesting and ask for their opinions.

Unit Wrap-Up

1. Work in small groups. Discuss the situation and do the activities. Then share your results with the class.

You work in the marketing department of a company that makes backpacks. Your group is in charge of coming up with a marketing campaign for a new backpack design. The targeted consumers are the students in your school.

1. *Conduct a marketing survey*: Find out what kinds of ads appeal to the targeted consumers. Think about the information that you need to know. Then create a list of survey questions that will help you obtain this information. Survey students outside of class and compile your findings. What type of ads will you use? Why?

2. *Plan the advertising placement*: Decide together where to place the ads. Think about where students go, when they go there, and why they go there. Make a list of possible placement areas and give reasons for your choices.

2. Work in small groups. Look at two magazines: one for women and one for men. Discuss the questions and share your answers with the class.

Find an ad for the same type of product in both magazines, for example, skin-care products.

1. What are some of the differences in the ads?

2. How does the ad in the men's magazine appeal to men?

3. How does the ad in the women's magazine appeal to women?

4. If the product is traditionally female, how does the company market it to men? If it is traditionally male, how does the company market it to women?

Find an ad with no counterpart in the other magazine. How could the company market this product to the other gender? List some ideas.

Notes: _____

_____

_____

_____

unit
2

SOCIOLOGY

sociology \ˌsoʊsiˈɑləʤi\ The study of human societies
and social behavior

Chapter 3 — Work Habits in the United States

CHAPTER GOALS

- Learn about current trends in U.S. work habits
- Learn a Listening Strategy: Recognize lecture language that signals a transition between ideas
- Learn a Note-taking Strategy: Use symbols to stand for words and ideas
- Learn a Discussion Strategy: Interrupt and ask for clarification during a discussion

Build Background Knowledge

Think about the topic

1. **Look at the picture of an American at work. Then discuss the questions below in pairs.**

1. How many different things is this man doing?
2. Does this image give a true idea about work habits in the U.S.? Why or why not? Is it different for men and women?

2. Read this article about the choices some people have made to balance work and life.

Life's Labors

At the beginning of the twenty-first century, many people in the United States are better off than ever—they are healthier, wealthier, and better educated than at any other time in history. When we **analyze** work **trends** in the U.S., however, we see that Americans also work longer hours, work more jobs, and have less free time. Here are the stories of some of the people struggling with these issues.

Two aspiring actors in Los Angeles

Lisa and Harry Robles are trying to find success in the city of dreams. Like many actors, they moved to L.A. to pursue film and TV careers. Also like many actors, their income from acting does not meet their needs. To fill the gap, they **juggle** a variety of part-time jobs. This situation is made more difficult by the fact that they are the parents of two young children. Playing the **role** of parent along with their various other roles—in front of the camera and in real life—is tough, but they say it's worth it. They are following their dreams and believe that they will succeed eventually. For now, though, they have little free time. Their daily schedules are busy and complicated, and the whole family has learned to be very **efficient** with time, energy, and money.

A dot-com CFO in New York

Rupert Kinnaird has spent the past two years working for an Internet-based, or dot-com, company. Rupert loves his job, but he feels a lot of **pressure** to perform well because the company is still new and growing. His title is Chief Financial Officer, but it **turns out** that he plays many roles within his small company. Usually, he works 80 to 90 hours a week. This schedule has put tremendous strain on his relationships with his friends and family. He could easily change jobs and choose a **workplace** with regular hours, but he finds the Internet world fun and exciting. He also likes the financial rewards. Rupert claims that his **values** have not changed—friends and family are still the most important things in his life. For right now, though, he wants to focus on his career. His job keeps him busy, but it also makes him happy.

3. Answer the questions about the reading on page 25. Then discuss your answers with a partner.

1. What are some of the things that make Lisa and Harry's life difficult?

2. What are some of the things that make Rupert's life difficult?

3. What do all the people in the article have in common?

4. Match the words with their definitions. Look back at the article on page 25 to check your answers.

_____ 1. analyze   **a.** expectations that cause someone to feel worried or nervous

_____ 2. trend   **b.** the room or building where you work.

_____ 3. juggle   **c.** working well, quickly, and without wasting time, energy, or effort

_____ 4. role   **d.** to keep two or more activities in progress at the same time

_____ 5. efficient   **e.** the function someone has in a particular situation or activity

_____ 6. pressure   **f.** beliefs about what is important in life

_____ 7. workplace   **g.** to look closely at a situation in order to try to explain it

_____ 8. values   **h.** the way a situation is developing or changing

5. Circle the phrase with a similar meaning to the underlined idiom.

Pedro and Cecilia moved to Florida because they wanted a quieter life, but it turns out that they are busier now than they were in New York.
a. it is surprising   **b.** it is true   **c.** it is nice

6. Discuss these questions in a small group. Share your answers with the class.

1. The stories in the reading show examples of the growing trend in the U.S. toward being busier and working more. Is this trend true for people you know? Give examples to support your opinion.

2. The people in the reading seem to enjoy their lives even though they feel a lot of pressure. Do you think that most people enjoy their work?

7. With a partner, write down three things in your notebook that you have learned so far about work trends in the U.S.

Prepare To Listen And Take Notes

1. To help you understand the listening strategy, discuss the situation below and answer the question.

You are in a large university classroom listening to a two-hour lecture. The professor talks about one idea and then quickly moves to another idea. This happens over and over again. What might be difficult about this situation?

Listening Strategy

Recognize Lecture Language for Transitions
Professors use a variety of expressions throughout a lecture to signal a new idea, or the end of one idea and the beginning of a new idea. Think of these transitions as road signs that help you find your way.

Listen for transitions—the expressions that help you follow the flow of ideas in a lecture.

Transition lecture language

2. Read the expressions that signal a new idea or topic. Can you add others to the list?

Let me start with . . .	Now . . .
Next, let's talk about . . .	First, let's look at . . .
I want to focus on . . .	What I want to discuss now is . . .

_____

_____

3. Read the expressions that signal the end of one idea and the beginning of a new idea. Can you add others to the list?

Now that we have talked about _____, let's talk about . . .
Let's move on to . . .
That's enough about _____. Let's go to the next point.

_____

_____

Recognize lecture language

4. Read the excerpt from a lecture about work habits. Then underline the lecture language that signals a transition.

Marriage and work is an interesting topic, so let me start with the point that married couples have reacted in a variety of ways to the pressures they feel when both the husband and wife work. We've seen that it's a struggle for some couples, and somehow other couples can make it work. Let's move on to some of the polling data I collected with my colleagues last summer so that we can discover some of the reasons for these reactions.

5. Listen to the lecture about the work lives of three family members. Match the name of each person to the description of her work experience.

_____ **1.** Dina   **a.** She has never worked.

_____ **2.** Laura   **b.** She has worked in a fast food restaurant and in an office.

_____ **3.** Maria   **c.** She works in a law firm.

6. Listen to the lecture again. As you listen, write down the lecture language that signals a transition from one idea to another. Then listen once more and write down the idea that follows the transition.

1. Transition lecture language: _____

_____

New idea: _____

2. Transition lecture language: _____

_____

New idea: _____

3. Transition lecture language: _____

_____

New idea: _____

4. Transition lecture language: _____

_____

New idea: _____

Use Symbols
The average professor speaks at a rate of about 125 words a minute—too fast to write down every word. Using symbols will help you keep up with the professor's lecture. Use symbols in place of full words and phrases in order to write down ideas more quickly.

Use symbols

7. Look at these commonly used symbols. Can you add others to the list?

=	equals, is the same	#	number
≠	is not the same	w/	with
>	is more than	w/out	without
<	is less than	+	and
♂	man	↓	to go down, decrease, lower
♀	woman	↑	to go up, increase, higher
△	changing	!	(to mark importance)

_____   _____

_____   _____

8. Read these sentences from a lecture on work habits. Take notes using symbols to represent words and ideas.

1. It is important to know that the number of Internet businesses is increasing every day.

   # Internet businesses ↑ every day—! _____

2. One major change is that business today is international—it's not the same as it was 30 years ago.

   _____

3. Many men and women are employed and taking care of children.

   _____

4. Companies try to stay competitive in two ways: They try to have lower costs than other companies and they try to maximize production so that they can make more money.

   _____

   _____

Listen and Take Notes

Make predictions

▷ p. 8

1. Before the lecture, think about everything you have learned and discussed on the topic of work habits in the U.S. What do you expect to learn more about in the lecture? Write three predictions below. Compare your predictions with a partner.

   1. _____

   2. _____

   3. _____

Follow the lecture

▷ symbols, p. 29

2. Now follow the lecture and take notes using symbols to represent words and ideas. Remember to listen for the lecture language that signals a transition.

Topic: _____

Aspects of work habits research _____

_____

Research on how U.S. people work _____

_____

Reasons people feel busy _____

_____

_____

_____

In the workplace _____

_____

Additional point _____

_____

_____

3. How well were you able to recognize the lecture language? Circle the answer that best describes you. Explain your answer.

I was able to recognize the change from one idea to another _____ .

   a. all of the time   **b.** most of the time   **c.** sometimes   **d.** not often

4. Use your notes to answer these questions.

  1. What did the researchers find out about the amount of work that people feel they are doing?

    _____

    _____

    _____

  2. What are the three reasons for the increased feeling of busyness among working people today?

    _____

    _____

    _____

  3. What is the big change in the workplace that is causing workers to feel busier?

    _____

    _____

    _____

  4. Although people in the U.S. are busier, they like their jobs. Why is this true?

    _____

    _____

    _____

5. Were you able to answer the questions in Exercise 4 using the information in your notes? Compare your notes with a few other students. Discuss the differences and help each other fill in any missing information. Complete your notes.

6. Work with a partner and take turns. Review your notes from the lecture. Then explain the main points of the lecture to your partner. Talk for 2-3 minutes only.

Discuss the Issues

Discussion Strategy

Interrupt and Ask for Clarification

It is normal to not understand everything you hear during a discussion. In most classrooms in the U.S., students are expected to take responsibility when they don't understand what the professor or a classmate says. During a discussion, politely interrupt and ask questions when you don't understand.

Interrupt and ask for clarification

1. Read the expressions for interrupting and asking for clarification. Can you add others to the lists?

Non-Verbal Ways to Interrupt

Make eye contact with the speaker

Make a small hand gesture

Raise your hand and wait to be called on

_____

_____

Phrases to Use for Interrupting

Excuse me, . . .

I'm sorry, . . .

Before we go on, . . .

_____

_____

Questions to Ask When You Don't Understand

Could you repeat that?

Could you say that again please?

Could you explain that?

What does that mean?

What does that word mean?

_____

_____

2. In groups of four, read the questions and discuss them. Keep the conversation going until every student has had a chance to practice interrupting and asking for clarification. Use your own ideas and experience or the ones given below.

1. What kind of work have you done? Where?

Possible ideas

office work	in a bank	part-time full-time
in a bookstore	in a restaurant	in a convenience store
babysitting	in a business	repair work

2. What kinds of technology do you (or will you) use at your job?

Possible ideas

computers	cell phones	fax machines
cash registers	digital photography	health-care equipment

3. Discuss these ideas from the lecture with your classmates. Remember to use the phrases for interrupting and asking for clarification.

1. One trend described in the lecture is that people feel busier because they have to juggle many responsibilities. Is this true for you?

2. The lecture describes people in the U.S. as being very busy when they work. In your opinion, what are some of the positive effects of this and what are some of the negative effects?

3. According to the lecture, new technological developments have made it necessary for workers to "think and talk" at the same time. Is this true for you? Would you like to work this way? Why or not?

4. Look back at your notes. What was another idea in the lecture that you found important and interesting? Tell the class why you think it is important or interesting and ask for their opinions.

Chapter 4 | Leisure Time in the United States

CHAPTER GOALS

- Learn about current trends in U.S. leisure activity
- Learn a Listening Strategy: Recognize lecture language that signals a definition
- Learn a Note-taking Strategy: Use abbreviations to stand for words and ideas
- Learn a Discussion Strategy: Ask for more information during a discussion

Build Background Knowledge

Think about the topic

1. Read this survey about leisure time activities in the U.S. Then discuss the questions below in pairs.

The American Time Use Survey		
People aged 15 or over who report doing some amount of daily leisure activity **96%**	People 15-24 years	5.5 hours per day
	People 25-54 years	4 hours per day
	People 65 years and older	7.2 hours per day

1. Why does the amount of time spent on leisure vary with age?

2. For each age range, is this enough leisure time or too much? Why?

3. Do you think the finding in the chart is about right for your age group? How much time do you spend on leisure activities each day?

2. Read this article about trends in the way people spend their leisure time.

All or Nothing: Current Trends in Leisure Time

Every year since 1995, the Harris Poll, a **survey** group, has asked Americans, average age 25, to name their two or three favorite leisure time activities. Their goal is to identify trends in favorite leisure activities over time. The findings for 2003 are typical of the answers gathered every year so far.

The information gathered in the Harris survey shows the types of activities that people in the U.S. do in their leisure time. It does not, however, show the *ways* in which they do them. These stories of individuals show two different trends.

Multitask: The "All" Approach

Hamilton Lim represents the trend toward multitasking. He works sixty hours a week in the financial district in San Francisco and has a wife and two children. He lives his life at a fast **pace** and doesn't have much time for himself. His leisure time is at five in the morning. Exercising is Hamilton's method of **relaxation**. Working out at his gym on the Stairmaster helps him stay healthy and avoid getting **stressed out**. While he is exercising, however, Hamilton also likes to read the newspaper and watch the weather report on TV. Hamilton wants to get the most value from his leisure time, so he **multitasks** as much as possible. He feels that multitasking gives him the relaxation he needs but also prepares him for his day.

No-brainer: The "Nothing" Approach

Like Hamilton Lim, Sam Bronsky also has almost no time for himself. He works three jobs and rarely has a day off. When he does manage to get a little free time, he wants to escape from his **exhausting** schedule and get out of the city. He likes to **hang out** on the beach with friends or go fishing. When he is not able to go away, he enjoys gardening in his back yard. Sam calls his leisure time preferences **no-brainer** activities. They allow him to recover from his stressful work schedule and relax, but they do not require him to think about work or daily life.

For most people, these two approaches overlap. They may multitask in the evening and do no-brainer activities on the weekend. Think of leisure time as a line, with *multitasking* at one end and *no-brainer* at the other end. Where do you stand?

FAVORITE LEISURE ACTIVITIES, 2003	
Reading	24%
Watching TV	17%
Spending time with family	17%
Fishing	9%
Movie-going	7%
Playing team sports	6%
Exercising	6%
Gardening	6%

3. Answer the questions about the article on page 35. Then discuss your answers with a partner.

1. How does Hamilton Lim spend his leisure time?

2. How does Sam Bronsky spend his leisure time?

4. Circle the answer that correctly completes the definition of the word. Look back at the article on page 35 to check your answers.

1. A <u>survey</u> is a set of questions that helps researchers _____ people's opinions or behavior.

    a. find out about   **b.** form

2. <u>Pace</u> is the _____ at which something happens or is done.

    a. direction   **b.** speed

3. <u>Relaxation</u> is a way of feeling calm and _____ yourself.

    a. bored with   **b.** enjoying

4. To feel <u>stressed-out</u> means you are so _____ that you cannot relax.

    a. worried and tired   **b.** happy and tired

5. <u>Multitasking</u> means doing _____ at a time.

    a. only one thing   **b.** more than one thing

6. Something that is <u>exhausting</u> makes you feel _____ tired.

    a. extremely   **b.** a little

7. A <u>no-brainer</u> activity is something that needs _____ thought and attention.

    a. very little   **b.** a lot of

5. Circle the phrase with a similar meaning to the underlined idiom.

After the kids leave for school, Maggie Lim likes to <u>hang out</u> for a while and have a cup of tea before she starts her busy day.

a. do household chores   **b.** not do very much

6. Discuss these questions in a small group. Share your answers with the class.

1. Do you think the results of the Harris survey are generally true for the people you know? If the Harris Poll did this survey in your school, what other activities might appear on the list?

2. In your personal leisure time, are you more like Hamilton or Sam?

7. With a partner, write down three things in your notebook that you have learned so far about leisure time in the United States.

 p. 5

Prepare to Listen and Take Notes

1. To help you understand the listening strategy, discuss the situation below and answer the question.

Experts estimate that students learn up to 1,000 new words per year from reading and lectures. How can a student prepare for receiving new words during a lecture?

Listening Strategy

Recognize Lecture Language that Signals a Definition
Professors often use new words as they explain new information or ideas. They also use a variety of expressions to present definitions for those words.
Listen for the words and expressions that professors use to signal a definition.

Definition lecture language

2. Read the expressions that signal a definition. Can you add others to the list?

that is, …	X means _____
in other words, . . .	What I mean by X is _____
X, or _____	What I mean when I say X is _____
X, meaning _____	_____
by X, I mean _____	_____
X is the term for _____	_____

Another common signal for a definition is a rhetorical question. Rhetorical questions are given for the purpose of preparing the listener for the answer. They are not questions that the professor wants students to answer:
What do I mean by X? Well, I mean _____
What is X? X is _____

Recognize lecture language

3. Read the excerpt from a lecture about leisure activities. Underline and label the phrase to be defined, the lecture language that signals the definition, and the definition.

People who take the no-brainer approach to leisure time like to spend time on things that are a piece of cake, that is, things that are not too challenging. These kinds of activities, like watching TV, fishing, and sunbathing, allow them to spend time in a restful way.

People who multitask spend their time doing many things at once. They think that this is an efficient way to spend the little free time that they have. These people really do not like to fritter away their time. What I mean by fritter away their time is waste their time. The idea of wasting time is not a relaxing concept for them.

In fact, one of the things that we notice about multitaskers is that they are very thrifty, . . . thrifty in how they use their time. By thrifty, I mean that they use their time carefully without wasting it.

4. Listen to the lecture about how four different people spend their leisure time. Match the name of each person to the type of leisure activity he or she enjoys.

_____ **1.** Lily   **a.** nothing

_____ **2.** Marvin   **b.** skateboarding

_____ **3.** Taka   **c.** play and watch soccer

_____ **4.** Jo   **d.** bungee jumping

5. Listen to the lecture again. As you listen, write down the lecture language that signals a definition. Then listen once more and write down the definition.

1. Word: Findings

Lecture language: _____

Definition: _____

2. Word: Charisma

Lecture language: _____

Definition: _____

3. Word: Bungee Jumping

Lecture language: _____

Definition: _____

4. Word: Fakie

Lecture language: _____

Definition: _____

5. Word: Zilch

Lecture language: _____

Definition: _____

Note-taking Strategy

Use Abbreviations

The average professors speaks at a rate of about 125 words a minute—too fast to write every word. Using abbreviations along with symbols will help you keep up with the professor's lecture. Use abbreviations in place of full words in order to write down ideas more quickly.

Use abbreviations

6. Look at these commonly used abbreviations. Can you add others to the list?

adv	advantage	e.g.	example	info	information
avg	average	est	estimate	max	maximum
aprox	approximately	esp	especially	min	minimum
btwn	between	etc.	etcetera	pg	page
cont	continued	i.d.	identity	pop	population
diff	difference, different	i.e.	in other words	vs.	versus
ea	each	imp	important		

_____   _____   _____

_____   _____   _____

7. Read the sentences from a lecture on leisure. Take notes using abbreviations to represent words and ideas

1. Each year the Harris Poll conducts a survey of Americans. For each survey that they conduct, they focus on different parts of the population.

   Harris Poll ea yr conducts survey of Ams. ea survey focuses on diff pop

2. This leisure survey focused on people with the average age of 25. All of the surveys help them identify important trends.

   _____

   _____

3. Experts research how the American population spends leisure time versus how they spend their work time.

   _____

   _____

4. Experts try to get information on how different age groups and genders spend leisure time.

   _____

   _____

Listen and Take Notes

Make predictions

▷ p. 8

1. **Before the lecture, think about everything you have learned and discusssed on the topic of leisure time in the U.S. What do you expect to learn more about in the lecture? Write three predictions below. Compare your predictions with a partner.**

   1. _____

   2. _____

   3. _____

Follow the lecture

▷ abbreviations, p. 39

2. **Now follow the lecture and take notes using abbreviations and symbols. Remember to listen for the lecture language that signals a definition.**

Topic: _____

How people spend their time at work _____

_____

First way people organize their leisure time _____

_____

Reasons _____

_____

Survey results _____

_____

Second way that people organize their leisure time _____

_____

Reasons _____

_____

_____

_____

_____

3. How well were you able to recognize the lecture language? Circle the answer that best describes you. Explain your answer.

I was able to recognize the lecture language for definitions _____.
a. all of the time   **b.** most of the time   **c.** sometimes   **d.** not often

4. Use your notes to answer these questions.

1. What are two reactions that people have to the increased feeling of busyness?

    _____

    _____

    _____

2. What is one example of how people multitask during leisure time?

    _____

    _____

    _____

3. What are three examples of no-brainer leisure activity choices?

    _____

    _____

    _____

4. Why do some people become couch potatoes?

    _____

    _____

    _____

Assess your notes

 p. 9

5. Were you able to answer the questions in Exercise 4 using the information in your notes? Compare your notes with a few other students. Discuss the differences and help each other fill in any missing information. Complete your notes.

Summarize the lecture

 p. 19

6. Work with a partner and take turns. Review your notes from the lecture. Then explain the main points of the lecture to your partner. Talk for 2-3 minutes only.

Discuss the Issues

Discussion Strategy

Ask for More Information
During a discussion, you might be interested in an idea and want to understand it better, or you might need to know more about it for a test or an assignment. In a discussion, politely ask questions to get more information about a point or idea.

Ask for more information

1. **Read the expressions for asking for more information. Can you add others to the list?**

Could you explain more about . . . ?   How does that work?
Could you tell me more about . . .?   What do you mean by that?
Give me an example of . . .?   What's an example of that?
Could you explain that in more detail?
What's the difference between _____ and _____ ?

_____

_____

_____

Practice asking for more information

2. In groups of four, read the questions and discuss them. Keep the conversation going until every student has had a chance to practice asking for more information. Use your own ideas or the ones given below.

1. What do you and your friends do in your leisure time?

   Possible Ideas

play sports	watch TV	hang out with friends
drive around	shop	listen to music read

2. What are some of the differences between reading and watching TV?

   Possible Ideas

Reading	**Watching TV**
quiet	lively
have to use your imagination	a lot of choice
nice for spending time alone	feels social

Discuss the ideas in the lecture

3. Discuss these ideas from the lecture with your classmates. Remember to use the phrases for asking for more information.

1. Think of another culture that you are familiar with. Do people in that culture spend their leisure time in similar ways to people in the United States or very differently? Explain your answer.

2. The lecture describes Americans as busy when they do leisure activities. In your opinion, what are some of the positive effects of this and what are some of the negative effects?

3. The lecture says that some people react to a busy work life by being couch potatoes in their leisure time. In your opinion, what are some of the positive effects of this and what are some of the negative effects?

4. Look back at your notes. What was another idea in the lecture that you found important and interesting? Tell the class why you think it is important or interesting and ask for their opinions.

Unit Wrap-Up

1. **Work in small groups. Assign each person in the group a different age group to survey: 13-17, 18-22, 23-30, 31-40, over 40. Survey these age groups outside of class using the survey questions below. Discuss the results in your group. Draw three to five general conclusions based on your findings. Then compare your findings with the other groups.**

   1. What do you usually do in your leisure time?

   2. How much time do you spend on leisure time in a week?

   3. How much money do you usually spend each week or month on leisure activities?

2. **Discuss the following information about leisure in the workplace. As a class, brainstorm the pros and cons of this approach. Then divide the class into two parts and debate the pros and cons.**

   Some companies in the United States try to make leisure activities available to employees in the workplace. They provide tennis courts, swimming pools, fitness equipment, pool tables, and outdoor parks for employee use. Some give employees a day off to go to an amusement park together.

3. **Interview working people who are at least 50 years old. Find out what types of technology they used prior to 1980 and what technology they have used since 1980. How have changes in technology affected their work and their lives?**

   Notes: _____

   _____

   _____

   _____

   _____

   _____

   _____

   _____

unit
3

SCIENCE

science \'saɪəns\ A system of knowledge concerned with the physical world and its phenomena

Science and Pleasure: Choosing What We Eat

CHAPTER GOALS

- Learn about some of the reasons behind food choice
- Learn a Listening Strategy: Recognize lecture language that signals an example
- Learn a Note-taking Strategy: Organize key material in visual form
- Learn a Discussion Strategy: Agree and disagree during a discussion

Think about the topic

Build Background Knowledge

1. Look at the cartoon. Then discuss the questions below in pairs.

"I'm going to order a broiled skinless chicken breast, but I want you to bring me lasagna and garlic bread by mistake."

© 1998 Randy Glasbergen.

1. What are some of the differences between the food that the woman is going to order and the food that she really wants to eat?

2. Why do you think that she chooses one but hopes to eat the other?

The Food Guide Pyramid

The **U.S. Department of Agriculture** is a government agency that researches the **diet** of Americans and makes **recommendations** about the type of food Americans should eat. To make these suggestions they study the **nutrition** that the human body needs for energy and growth—the amount of vitamins, proteins, and minerals that people should take into their bodies every day. Once they understand the nutritional needs, they use this information as the **source** for recommendations about food. Their recommendations tell people what food they should eat to meet their nutritional requirements. The USDA hopes that their recommendations will **influence** what Americans eat.

In 1992, the USDA created The Food Guide Pyramid to share these recommendations with people. The Pyramid condensed 70 pages of recommendations into an image that was clear and useful to the public. The Pyramid helped people choose what and how much to eat in order to get the nutrients they needed.

In 2005, the USDA updated the pyramid so that each person can now get personalized advice about diet and exercise. The new, online MyPyramid, found at www.MyPyramid.gov, comes in 12 versions depending on a person's activity level and need for calories. Eric M. Bost, the Agriculture Department's undersecretary for food, nutrition, and consumer services, thinks that this new pyramid is a good idea because diet is a serious issue in the U.S. He said that 65% of adults ages 20 to 74 are overweight.

There is some **controversy** about the recommendations on the new pyramid. Some public health officials think that it should say more about the foods to avoid, not just the foods to choose.

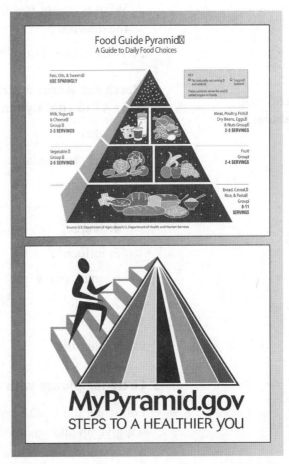

Others are happy to see that the recommended serving sizes are more specific. The **debate** continues as scientists, researchers, and the public voice their different opinions about MyPyramid.

Even though there is controversy and the recommendations are not complete, the USDA says that people should not use this as a reason to ignore the recommendations. The goal of the old and the new pyramid is to encourage people not to eat only for **pleasure**, but to think about how to get the nutrients and exercise that their bodies need. True, it might be hard to follow the recommendations, but people should not **give up** and eat whatever they want, whenever they want.

3. Answer the questions about the article on page 47. Then discuss your answers with a partner.

1. What is the purpose of the Food Guide Pyramid?

2. What is one of the differences between the old Food Guide Pyramid and the new one?

3. What is one controversy about the recommendations on the pyramid?

4. Match the words with their definitions. Look back at the article on page 47 to check your answers.

___ **1.** diet   **a.** the right type of food for good health

___ **2.** recommendation   **b.** the place where something starts or comes from

___ **3.** nutrition   **c.** discussion on a subject that people disagree about

___ **4.** source   **d.** the type of food that someone usually eats

___ **5.** influence   **e.** the feeling of being happy or satisfied

___ **6.** controversy   **f.** advice based on knowledge of the subject

___ **7.** debate   **g.** to effect the way something or someone behaves

___ **8.** pleasure   **h.** strong disagreement in society about an idea

5. Circle the phrase with a similar meaning to the underlined idiom.

Following the USDA recommendations can be confusing, but people should not <u>give up</u> and ignore the recommendations completely.

a. stop trying   **b.** ask questions   **c.** argue

6. Discuss these questions in a small group. Share your answers with the class.

1. In what situations would you consider recommendations from experts about the food you eat? Describe the situations.

2. Are there times when you don't think about your diet at all and just eat whatever you want? When? Why?

 p. 5

7. With a partner, write down three things in your notebook that you have learned so far about nutrition and the food pyramid.

Prepare to Listen and Take Notes

1. To help you understand the listening strategy, discuss the situation below and answer the question.

Imagine someone asks you, "What is a carbohydrate?" Without using a dictionary, what is a quick and easy way to communicate the meaning?

Listening Strategy

Recognize Lecture Language for Examples
Professors use examples throughout their lectures. These examples of specific things help students understand general ideas.

Listen for the words and expressions that professors use to signal an example.

Example lecture language

2. Read the expressions that signal an example. Can you add others to the list?

For Actual Examples

For example, . . .
Take X, for example.
Here is a perfect example of what I mean.
Here are some examples of . . .
Let's look at a couple of examples of . . .

To illustrate, let's look at . . .
For instance, . . .
Such as . . .
Like . . .

For Hypothetical (Unreal) Examples

Let's say . . .
Take something like . . .

_____

_____

Recognize lecture language

3. Read the excerpt from a lecture on the Food Guide Pyramid. Underline and label the lecture language that signals an example and the examples.

· ·

On the new updated pyramid, we see something new. Each person can get personalized recommendations about diet and exercise. Let's look at what they recommend. For moderate exercise, here are some examples of the kind of physical activity that is recommended: walking quickly (about 3 1/2 miles per hour), hiking, gardening/yard work, dancing, golf, bicycling.

But, some physical activities are not intense enough to help you meet the recommendations. They are activities like these — the walking that you do while grocery shopping, and doing light household chores. Although you are moving, these activities do not increase your heart rate.

· ·

4. Listen to the excerpt from a lecture on the Food Guide Pyramid. Match the terms that the professor uses with the examples.

— **1.** Orange band   **a.** Vegetables

— **2.** Green band   **b.** Fruit

— **3.** Red band   **c.** Grains

— **4.** Yellow band   **d.** Oils/Fats

5. Listen to the excerpt again. As you listen, write down the lecture language that signals an example. Then listen once more and write down the examples.

1. Idea: Grains

Example lecture language: _____

Example: _____

2. Idea: Vegetables

Example lecture language: _____

Example: _____

3. Idea: Fruit

Example lecture language: _____

Example: _____

4. Idea: Oils/Fats

Example lecture language: _____

Example: _____

5. Idea: Milk

Example lecture language: _____

Example: _____

6. Idea: Meat and Beans

Example lecture language: _____

Example: _____

Note-taking Strategy

Use a Visual Form
Sometimes, it is easier to record and remember an idea when you represent it as a picture or some sort of graphic image. In your notes, record information in a visual form to remind yourself how the points relate to each other.

To represent a progression or flow of information, put the key idea in the center at the top of the page. Then put points and examples into columns and connect them with arrows (← ↑ ↓ →) and plus signs (+) to show relationships.

Take notes in visual form

6. Read the transcript from a lecture on the process of digestion. Then look at one student's notes from the lecture. Answer the questions below.

The process of digestion involves many of the body's organs, such as the stomach, intestines, liver, and kidneys. The first step of digesting food happens in our mouths. We chew and swallow. Swallowed food is then pushed into the esophagus through the throat, which is between the mouth and the esophagus. The food enters the stomach from the esophagus. The stomach has three things to do. First, the stomach must store the swallowed food and liquid. Then it mixes the food and liquid with digestive juices. The final task of the stomach is to empty its contents into the small intestine.

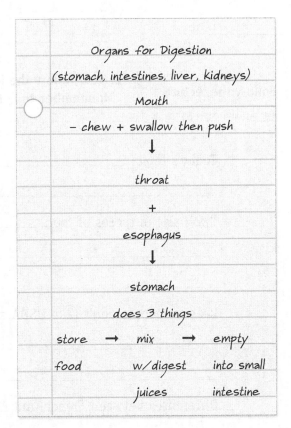

1. What was the main point of the lecture? How do you know this?

2. How does the student represent examples?

3. How do you know the order of the steps?

4. How does the student show that the stomach has three tasks?

7. Read this excerpt from a lecture on digestion. Take notes in your notebook using a visual form.

Digestion involves three processes. These are, first, the mixing of food; second, the movement of food through the digestive tract; and third, the chemical breakdown of the large molecules of food into smaller molecules. Digestion begins in the mouth, when we chew and swallow, and is completed in the small intestine.

Listen and Take Notes

Make predictions

▷ p. 8

1. Before the lecture, think about everything you have learned and discussed on the topic of nutrition and eating. What do you expect to learn more about in the lecture? Write three predictions below. Compare your predictions with a partner.

1. _____

2. _____

3. _____

Follow the lecture

▷ visual form, p. 51

2. Now follow the lecture and take notes, using a visual form if helpful. Remember to listen for the lecture language that signals an example.

Today's topic: _____

_____

Two basic purposes of food _____

_____

_____

Reasons people don't take USDA advice on diet _____

_____

_____

Differences between French and American attitudes toward food ____

_____

_____

Reasons for the French attitude toward food _____

_____

_____

Reasons for the American attitude toward food _____

_____

_____

3. How well were you able to recognize the lecture language? Circle the statement that best describes you. Explain your answer.

I was able to recognize when the professor gave examples _____.
a. all of the time   **b.** some of the time   **c.** none of the time   **d.** not sure

4. Use your notes to answer these questions.

1. What are the two basic purposes of food?

_____

_____

_____

2. Why don't people always take the recommendations of the USDA Dietary Guidelines?

_____

_____

_____

3. What did the specific example of potato chips tell you about nutritional information in general?

_____

_____

_____

4. Name at least three of the differences between the French attitude toward food and the American attitude toward food?

_____

_____

_____

Assess your notes

 p. 9

5. Were you able to answer the questions in Exercise 4 using the information in your notes? Compare your notes with a few other students. Discuss the differences and help each other fill in any missing information. Complete your notes.

Summarize the lecture

 p. 19

6. Work with a partner and take turns. Review your notes from the lecture. Then explain the main points of the lecture to your partner. Talk for 2-3 minutes only.

Discuss The Issues

Discussion Strategy

Agreeing and Disagreeing
During a group discussion, you might want to agree with another student and build on the point, or disagree with another student and explain why. This type of exchange is good because it indicates how well you understand the topic. Use expressions to agree or disagree with others in a discussion.

Agree and disagree

1. **Read the expressions for agreeing and disagreeing. Can you add others to the list?**

   To agree with others
   I agree with _____ , . . .
   That's a good point, . . .
   I agree with _____'s point, . . .
   S/he's right, . . .
   I think _____ has the right idea, . . .

   To disagree with others
   I'm afraid I don't agree, . . .
   I'm sorry, but I have to disagree, . . .
   I disagree with _____ , . . .
   No, I don't think that's true, . . .
   I see your point, but . . .
   Perhaps you're right about _____, but I can't agree with you on . . .

Practice agreeing and disagreeing

2. In groups of four, read the questions and discuss them. Keep the conversation going until every student has had a chance to practice using the language for agreeing and disagreeing. Use your own ideas and opinions or the ones given below.

1. Do you think it is necessary to eat breakfast in the morning?

Possible Ideas

Necessary	Not Necessary
gives you energy	makes you sleepy
keeps you feeling full	wastes time
helps you concentrate and think	too sugary

2. Is American food healthy or unhealthy?

Possible Ideas

Healthy	Unhealthy
lots of fresh vegetables	big portions
organic food	lots of high fat food
low-salt choices	fast food

Discuss the ideas in the lecture

3. Discuss these ideas from the lecture with your classmates. Remember to use the phrases for agreeing and disagreeing.

1. Which do you think is more important to consider when choosing your food, nutritional needs or pleasure? Why?

2. Where do you get information about the health quality of food? Do you ever find this information confusing? Why?

3. The professor wraps up the lecture by saying that how we eat and how we feel about eating is just as important as what we eat. Explain what you think the professor means. Do you agree or disagree with this opinion? Why?

4. Look back at your notes. What was another idea in the lecture that you found important and interesting? Tell the class why you think it is important or interesting and ask for their opinions.

Chapter 6 | Unique Solutions to Pollution

CHAPTER GOALS
- Learn about some unique solutions to pollution
- Learn a Listening Strategy: Recognize lecture language that signals an explanation of an idea
- Learn a Note-Taking Strategy: Describe the graphics used in a lecture
- Learn a Discussion Strategy: Support your opinions during a discussion

Think about the topic

Build Background Knowledge

1. Look at the picture. Then discuss the questions below in pairs.

1. What are some forms of pollution? Does every urban area have every form? Why or why not?

2. What are some ways that government and the public can prevent or reduce pollution?

Read

2. **Read this magazine article about how children's health issues have inspired new pollution laws.**

The Effects of Air Pollution on Children

The average adult breathes over 3,000 gallons of air every day. When you compare body weight and the size of their lungs, children breathe even more. It is not surprising, then, that air pollution has a bigger negative **impact** on the children in any **population** than on the adults. Air pollution can cause breathing problems, disorders in the nervous system, and an increased risk of cancer later in life.

The American Lung Association **paints a picture** of why children are so affected by air pollution. Children are generally more active than adults. As a result, they breathe more rapidly and take more pollution deep into their lungs. Children also often breathe through their mouths, not through their noses. The mouth cannot filter out pollutants as well as the nose. Finally, children generally spend an average of 50 percent more time outdoors than adults, especially during summer months. Air pollution levels are highest in the summer.

In the past thirty years, programs to improve air **quality** have made **significant** progress in reducing air pollution in cities. Most of these air quality improvement programs have focused on getting **factories** to reduce the amount of pollution they put into the air. New programs, however, target air quality on a smaller scale. They want to improve the quality of air in children's daily lives. A good example of this is a new type of "No Smoking" law. Its goal is to reduce *secondhand smoke*—cigarette smoke in the air that others breathe in.

Experts say that secondhand smoke is just as dangerous outside as inside. More than seventy cities in the United States now prohibit smoking in public places—all public places. Los Angeles, California, and Columbus, Ohio, for example, have banned smoking in public parks. Smokers have to pay a fine of $100 to $250 for smoking in any public outdoor recreation area, including city parks, gardens, and sports fields.

Some city officials are in favor of the new laws because they want to reduce the amount of secondhand smoke that children breathe. Others want to help the environment in general. Most want both. "Those of us living in an urban environment are constantly exposing ourselves to toxic **substances**," a city health official in San Francisco, California, said. "Anything that cleans up our **environment**, I'm in favor of."

Unit 3 Science   **57**

3. Answer the questions about the article on page 57. Then discuss your answers with a partner.

1. Why are children more affected by air pollution than adults?

2. What is different about the new "No Smoking" laws?

3. What have cities done recently to improve air quality?

4. Circle the answer that correctly completes the definition of the word. Look back at the article on page 57 to check your answers.

1. To have an <u>impact</u> on someone or something means to have _____.

   a. an effect   **b.** an opinion

2. The <u>population</u> of an area is another way to say the _____ in that area.

   a. people   **b.** children

3. To measure the <u>quality</u> of something means learning how _____ it is.

   a. big or small   **b.** good or bad

4. When something is <u>significant</u>, it is _____.

   a. important   **b.** not important

5. A <u>factory</u> is a place where a company makes products in _____ quantities.

   a. large   **b.** small

6. A <u>substance</u> is _____ that has special characteristics.

   a. an idea or plan   **b.** a type of solid, liquid, or gas

7. The <u>environment</u> refers to the _____ around us.

   a. businesses, factories, and offices   **b.** air, water, and land

5. Circle the phrase with a similar meaning to the underlined idiom.

The increasing number of children with breathing problems and diseases <u>paints a picture</u> of the quality of the air in urban areas.

a. influences   **b.** describes

6. Discuss these questions in a small group. Share your answers with the class.

1. How do you feel about smoking outdoors? Do you think it is a problem? Why or why not?

2. Do you think that smoking increases the general air pollution in a city? Why or why not? Will banning outdoor smoking help a city's environment?

7. With a partner, write down three things in your notebook that you have learned so far about the problems caused by air pollution.

Prepare to Listen and Take Notes

1. To help you understand the listening strategy, discuss the situation below and answer the question.

Imagine that you are going to hear a lecture on the effects of air pollution on the environment. Which aspect of the lecture will help the class best understand the problem? Choose one.

    a. an example of pollution   **c.** a definition of pollution

    b. an explanation of pollution

Listening Strategy

> **Recognize Lecture Language for Explanations**
> Professors give explanations throughout lectures. They describe complex processes and ideas in a way that makes them easier to understand.
> Listen for the words and expressions that professors use to signal an explanation.

Explanation lecture language

2. Read the expressions that signal an explanation. Can you add others to the list?

Let me explain . . .	Let me clarify . . .
What I mean is . . .	Let's look at how this works. . . .
How does this work? . . .	I want to show you how _____ works. . . .
Let me spell this out. . . .	Let me show you what I mean. . . .
So I hope you can see how this explains _____ .	

_____

_____

Recognize lecture language

3. Read the excerpt from a lecture on the process of breathing. Underline and label the lecture language that signals an explanation and also the explanations.

....

Your lungs are complex organs. Let me explain what they do. They take a gas that your body needs to get rid of—carbon dioxide—and exchange it for a gas that your body can use—oxygen. In today's lecture we will take a close look at how your lungs work and how they keep your body's cells supplied with oxygen.

Your lungs' main job is to make oxygen available to your body and to remove other gases, such as carbon dioxide. This process is done 12 to 20 times per minute. Let me clarify how this process works. When you inhale air through your nose or mouth, air travels down the back of your throat (pharynx), passes through your voice box (larynx), and into your windpipe (trachea).

....

🎧 **4. Listen to the excerpt from a lecture on the ways that people respond to pollution. Match the type of response that the professor discusses to an example of the response.**

— **1.** respond personally   **a.** clean up rivers and beaches

— **2.** become involved in   **b.** buy environmentally friendly
      environmental organizations   office supplies

— **3.** respond at work   **c.** ride a bike

Listen for explanations

🎧 **5. Listen to the excerpt again. Write the lecture language that signals an explanation. Then listen once more and write down the explanation.**

1. Idea: They change their personal worlds

Explanation lecture language: _____

Explanation: _____

2. Idea: They become involved in environmental organizations

Explanation lecture language: _____

Explanation: _____

3. Idea: Businesses are concerned

Explanation lecture language: _____

Explanation: _____

4. Idea: They purchase office supplies that are more environmentally friendly

Explanation lecture language: _____

Explanation: _____

Note-taking Strategy

Describe the Visuals Used in a Lecture
Professors often include visuals like pictures, charts, and graphs in lectures to help make ideas clearer. Make sure that you describe the visual in your notes and write down important information about it.

6. Read the transcript from a lecture on how the lungs work and study the picture that the professor uses. Then, look at how one student represents the visual in her notes. Answer the questions below.

You breathe in through your nose and mouth. The air travels down through a large tube in your throat called the windpipe. Then it moves through large and small tubes in your lungs called bronchial tubes or airways. The airways in your lungs look something like an upside-down tree with many branches.

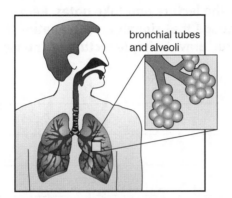

bronchial tubes and alveoli

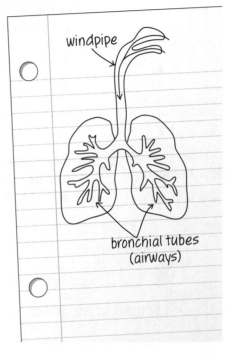

windpipe

bronchial tubes (airways)

1. How complex is the student's drawing? Do you think it took a lot of time to draw?

2. What labels did the student use? Did she use enough labels?

3. Is the drawing complete enough to be useful to the student for studying? Why or why not?

7. Look at the professor's visual again. Read the professor's explanation of a part of the lungs called the alveoli. Take notes that describe the visual and the ideas, including a simple drawing.

The smallest airways end in the alveoli: small, thin air sacs that are arranged in clusters like bunches of balloons. When you breathe in, the alveoli expand as air rushes in to fill the lungs. When you breathe out, the alveoli relax and air moves out of the lungs.

Listen and Take Notes

Make predictions

▷ p. 8

1. Before the lecture, think about everything you have learned and discussed on the topic of pollution. What do you expect to learn more about in the lecture? Write three predictions below. Compare your predictions with a partner.

1. _____

2. _____

3. _____

Follow the lecture

▷ describe visuals, p. 61

2. Now follow the lecture and take notes. Remember to listen for the lecture language that signals an explanation. Describe the graphics and, if helpful, draw a simple picture of the visuals.

Today's topic: _____

_____

Sources of air pollution _____

_____

_____

Sulfur dioxide _____

_____

_____

Health problems caused by air pollution _____

_____

_____

Benefits of trees _____

_____

_____

_____

_____

3. How well were you able to recognize the lecture language? Circle the answer that best describes you. Explain your answer.

I was able to recognize when the professor gave explanations _____ .
a. all of the time   **b.** some of the time   **c.** none of the time   **d.** not sure

4. Use your notes to answer these questions.

1. How is acid rain formed?

_____

_____

_____

2. What is one of the biggest sources of sulfur dioxide? Why?

_____

_____

_____

3. What are two of the ways that sulfur dioxide affects people and two ways it affects nature?

_____

_____

_____

4. What are three benefits of trees in the urban forest?

_____

_____

_____

5. Were you able to answer the questions in Exercise 4 using the information in your notes? Compare your notes with a few other students. Discuss the differences and help each other fill in any missing information. Complete your notes.

6. Work with a partner and take turns. Review your notes from the lecture. Then explain the main points of the lecture to your partner. Talk for 2-3 minutes only.

Discuss the Issues

Discussion Strategy

Support Your Opinion
Your opinions are more interesting and persuasive when you support them with details, examples, personal stories, and other information. Use expressions and phrasing to indicate that you can support your opinion.

Support your opinion

1. **Read the expressions and phrasing for supporting your opinion. Can you add others to the list?**

I think _____   Let me tell you why. . . .
                     Let me give you an example. . . .
                     and the reason is . . .
                     because . . .
                     for the following reasons: . . .
In my experience, that is/is not true. . . . (give one or more examples)

_____

_____

_____

**2. In groups of four, read the questions and discuss them. Keep the
conversation going until every student has had a chance to practice
giving an opinion and supporting it. Use your own ideas and opinions
or the ones given below.**

1. Should people be allowed to drive cars without restrictions in major
urban areas? Why or why not?

Yes	**No**
it's convenient	produces air pollution
it give you "alone time"	produces noise pollution
it's faster than public transportation	it causes traffic jams

2. Should people be allowed to smoke wherever they want?

Yes	**No**
people should have freedom of choice	smoking hurts others
smokers shouldn't be punished for	(especially children)
having an addiction	smoking is messy
it saves time (for example, smokers can	smoke smells bad
work rather than leave the building)	

**3. Discuss these ideas from the lecture with your classmates. Remember
to use the phrases for supporting your opinion.**

1. Have you or anyone you know been affected by air pollution? Describe
the effects.

2. Why don't people do more to help the environment? How can cities
persuade people to reduce pollution?

3. Imagine that there is a large piece of undeveloped land for sale in your
city. The city council is debating two proposals, or ideas, for what to do
with the land:

• Sell it for a lot of money to a developer who wants to build houses
and businesses on it. The money from the sale would allow the city to
clean up the river and create parkland along the riverbank.
• Sell it to an environmental group for less money. This group wants to
plant more trees on it and turn it into a nature preserve with hiking
trails and camping areas.

Discuss the two options and decide on one recommendation to give to the
city council.

4. Look back at your notes. What was another idea in the lecture that
you found important and interesting? Tell the class why you think it is
important or interesting and ask for their opinions.

1. **Find out more about pollution by researching one of these topics. Share your research findings with the class.**

   - a form of pollution other than air pollution—for example, noise, water, or light pollution

   - a pollutant other than SO_2—start by looking at the website for the Environmental Protection Agency, www.epa.gov.

2. **Go online and research ways in which people can make a difference in pollution reduction in their everyday lives. Find some ideas that are new to you and some that you can try in your own life. Share your findings with the class. Be sure to cite your sources so that others can read more on their own.**

3. **Visit the website www.MyPyramid.gov and do the activities below. Share your results and answers with the class.**

   - Look at the USDA's new diet and exercise recommendations. Enter information about your own age and level of activity and get the personalized recommendations.

   - Compare your current diet and level of exercise with what the USDA recommends. Do you agree with the recommendations? Why or why not?

   - Think about the changes you would have to make in your life to follow the USDA recommendations. How easy would this be for you? Do you plan to make the changes? Why or why not?

   Notes: _____

   _____

   _____

   _____

   _____

   _____

   _____

   _____

unit 4

MEDIA STUDIES

media studies \\'midiə 'stʌdiz\\ The study of the processes by which information is exchanged

Chapter 7 | Getting the News in the High-Tech Age

CHAPTER GOALS —
- Learn about the current trend away from newspaper news and toward Internet news
- Learn a Listening Strategy: Recognize lecture language that signals when information is important
- Learn a Note-taking Strategy: Highlight key ideas
- Learn a Discussion Strategy: Connect your ideas to other people's ideas in a discussion

Build Background Knowledge

Think about the topic

1. Look at the picture of people reading the news. Then discuss the questions below in pairs.

1. What are some of the ways that people get the news every day? How do you get the news?

2. Imagine that you hear about a natural disaster, such as a hurricane or earthquake, in your hometown. What would you do to get news about it? Explain.

2. Read this article about some of the ways that news has changed.

The Nature of News

What do people mean by the term "news"? More than a century ago, an editor at the *New York Sun* explained it this way: "If a dog bites a man, it's not news. If a man bites a dog, that's news." That statement is still true today—unusual things make the news. Conflicts and events that are very recent are also news. When famous people do something, that's news, too.

The way we get the news—the **media**—is undergoing tremendous change. For example, more and more people today have **access** to the Internet, where they can choose what type of news to look at. These days, people are choosing "news you can use." Rather than looking for **in-depth** news stories about events in the world, they want news about their own needs and concerns. People want **reliable** information about the traffic on the roads near their house, where to buy the cheapest plane tickets, or whether it's going to rain tomorrow. "News you can use" means **accurate** information that people can act on directly, by taking a different route to work, by buying a plane ticket online, or by changing their weekend plans.

Another **feature** of today's news is its focus on analysis. In the past, the news gave people information about individual events. Today, people depend on the news to **get informed** about how individual events happen together to affect the world, their work, or their lives. They want to know what's happening, but they also want to know what it means for their lives. News reporters are constantly searching for groups of events that signal new trends. For example, a reporter in Chicago went to several supermarkets in one week. He noticed that they were all offering free childcare for their customers. Shoppers could leave their children in a supervised play area while they shopped. The reporter did not report on one store and its new childcare feature. He reported on a new trend on the part of businesses to become more parent-friendly. This kind of news analysis helps people **keep up with** trends and better understand how to adapt to them.

The new emphasis on practical news applies to every type of news medium—TV, **print** media, radio, and especially the Internet. With so many media choices, there is almost no limit to the amount of "news you can use."

**3. Answer the questions about the article on page 69. Then discuss your
answers with a partner.**

1. What does the term "news you can use" mean?

2. What is the benefit of today's focus on news analysis?

3. What kind of news do reporters search for now? What is one example?

**4. Match the words with their definitions. Look back at the article on
page 69 to check your answers.**

_____ **1.** media	**a.** can be trusted
_____ **2.** access	**b.** find out about
_____ **3.** in-depth	**c.** TV, radio, newspapers, the Internet, as a group
_____ **4.** reliable	**d.** a way of entering or reaching
_____ **5.** accurate	**e.** with a lot of details
_____ **6.** feature	**f.** writing that is in books and newspapers
_____ **7.** get informed	**g.** an important or noticeable part of something
_____ **8.** print	**h.** careful and exact

5. Circle the phrase with a similar meaning to the underlined idiom.

Reading the newspaper every day helps people <u>keep up with</u> international,
national, and local events.

a. write down   **b.** continue to learn about   **c.** talk to people about

**6. Discuss these questions in a small group. Share your answers with
the class.**

1. When you pick up a newspaper or visit a news website, do you have
more interest in the news about world events or "news you can use"?
Why?

2. Which is more reliable, news in a newspaper or news on the Internet?
Why do you think so?

**7. With a partner, write down three things in your notebook that you
have learned so far about types of news.**

Prepare to Listen and Take Notes

1. **To help you understand the listening strategy, discuss the situation below and answer the question.**

   During a lecture, the professor says, "Now, let me repeat that." What should you do?
   a. Stop listening because you heard it already.
   b. Listen carefully because the information must be important.

Listening Strategy

> **Recognize Lecture Language that Signals Important Information**
> During a lecture, a professor will often communicate that he or she is making an important point and that you should pay special attention to it. When this happens, be sure to write the information down.
>
> Listen for the expressions that professors use to signal an important piece of information.

Lecture language for important information

2. **Read the expressions that signal an important piece of information. Can you add others to the list?**

   Listen to this: . . .   It's important to note that . . .
   This is important/key/crucial.   Pay attention to this: . . .
   You should write this down.   I want you to notice that . . .
   Let me repeat that, . . .   The bottom line is . . .
   I'll say that again, . . .   Here's the bottom line: . . .
   I want to point out/stress that . . .   This will be on the test.

   _____   _____

   _____   _____

Recognize lecture language

3. **Read the two excerpts from a lecture about the news media. Underline and label the lecture language that signals an important piece of information and also the information.**

   Excerpt 1
   All right. So far, we've been saying that people depend on the news to get informed about how events happen. I want to point out that the kind of news they look for is news that affects their lives directly. They want to know what's happening, but they also want to know what it means for their lives.

   Excerpt 2
   So, earlier I mentioned the role of reporters in gathering the news. And we said this discussion can apply to print, television, radio, and even Internet news. It's important to note that reporters are now looking for trends to report as news in all kinds of places—in stores, in the workplace, and even in schools.

4. Listen to an excerpt from a lecture about the news. Match the first part of each sentence with the correct second part.

— **1.** The number of hours people are online is

— **2.** Getting the news on the Internet is

— **3.** More people are using the Internet

a. to get information about big events.

b. 12½ hours per week.

c. the third most popular Internet activity.

5. Listen to the excerpt again. As you listen, write down the lecture language that signals an important piece of information. Then listen once more and write down the key point.

1. Important information lecture language: _____

Important information: _____

_____

2. Important information lecture language: _____

Important information: _____

_____

3. Important information lecture language: _____

Important information: _____

_____

4. Important information lecture language: _____

Important information: _____

_____

5. Important information lecture language: _____

Important information: _____

_____

6. Important information lecture language: _____

Important information: _____

_____

Highlighting Key Ideas
Some ideas in a lecture are very important. These can be facts, research results, examples, or definitions. As you listen, highlight the important points in your notes by marking them.

Highlight key ideas

6. Read the transcript from a lecture on Internet news. Then, look at one student's notes from the lecture. Answer the questions below.

There have been a number of recent studies on Internet use. The most recent study, from the University of Southern California, has the most accurate finding on Internet use. One important point they found out is that people go online an average of 12 and a half hours per week. Another important finding was that getting the news was the third most popular activity on the Internet. I'd like to point out a significant but more recent finding—there was a large increase in the number of people going to the Internet for big event news…that means news about war, or deaths of important people. So the point I want to stress the most is that the Internet is now the preferred source for big, current news stories for many people.

> Recent studies on Internet use
>
>   most recent—most accurate findings
>
>   Univ S. CA Int. use survey found
>
>   * people go online avg 12.5 hr/week
>   * getting news=3rd most popular activity
>
>   increase in # of Int. users for BIG EVENT news
>
>   war, deaths of important people, etc.
>
> → Internet = preferred source for big, current news

1. What ways did the student use to highlight information? Give examples.

2. What is the most important point in the lecture? How do you know?

7. Read this excerpt from a lecture on the changing nature of news. Take notes in your notebook using an informal outline and highlight key points and important information.

I want to stress that the news people want today is practical news. So, for example,… and this is important,… they want information about the weather and they want reliable traffic information. These are both practical kinds of news. The Internet is particularly important here for two reasons,… now write this down: it's often easier for people to access the Internet than a newspaper, and there is so much more of this kind of practical news available on the Internet.

Listen and Take Notes

Make predictions

▷ p. 8

1. Before the lecture, think about everything you have learned and discussed on the topic of getting the news. What do you expect to learn more about in the lecture? Write three predictions below. Compare your predictions with a partner.

   1. _____

   2. _____

   3. _____

Follow the lecture

▷ highlighting, p. 73

2. Now follow the lecture and take notes. Remember to listen for the lecture language that signals important information. Highlight important information as well.

Chapter 7 Getting the News in the High-Tech Age

Assess your comprehension

3. How well were you able to recognize the lecture language? Circle the answer that best describes you. Explain your answer.

I was able to recognize important information _____.

a. all the time   **b.** some of the time   **c.** none of the time   **d.** not sure

4. Use your notes to answer these questions.

1. What are the major trends that experts see in the way people get the news?

_____

_____

_____

2. Why did the professor mention the importance of young people?

_____

_____

_____

3. What are the three reasons people are choosing to get the news from the Internet?

_____

_____

_____

4. What are the three negative aspects of getting news from the Internet?

_____

_____

_____

Assess your notes

 p. 9

5. Were you able to answer the questions in Exercise 4 using the information in your notes? Compare your notes with a few other students. Discuss the differences and help each other fill in any missing information. Complete your notes.

Summarize the lecture

 p. 19

6. Work with a partner and take turns. Review your notes from the lecture. Then explain the main points of the lecture to your partner. Talk for 2-3 minutes only.

Discuss the Issues

Discussion Strategy

Connect Your Ideas to Others
During a discussion, you may have an idea that is related to something that someone else said. Use expressions to show that you understand how these ideas are connected and that you want to add your idea to the discussion.

Connecting your ideas to others

1. Read the expressions for connecting your ideas to others in a discussion. Can you add others to the list?

My idea is similar to Sam's.
My idea is a lot like Sam's idea.
I agree/disagree with what Sam said.
I agree/disagree with Sam that . . .
As Sam already said/pointed out, . . .
I'd like to go back to what Sam said. I . . .
Going back to what Sam said before, I . . .
Sam said _____, and I'd like to add . . .

_____

_____

Practice connecting ideas

2. In groups of four, read the questions and discuss them. Keep the conversation going until every student has had a chance to practice using the language for connecting ideas. Use your own ideas and opinions or the ones given below.

1. What kind of information can you get on the Internet?
   Possible Ideas

News	Health information
Shopping	Weather
Sports	Advice
Stock quotes	Local activities

2. Why is it important to get the news?
   Possible Ideas
   To help make decisions
   To be prepared for changes
   To know about the world
   To have something to talk about with friends

Discuss the ideas in the lecture

3. Discuss these ideas from the lecture with your classmates. Remember to use the phrases for connecting your ideas to other ideas.

1. The lecture points out that Internet news is current, complete, and interactive. When have you found this not to be true? Give examples.

2. What is one other positive or negative aspect of Internet news that you have noticed?

3. In your experience, do you feel young people know enough about current world events? How is the media involved in this?

4. Look back at your notes. What was another idea in the lecture that you found important and interesting? Tell the class why you think it is important or interesting and ask for their opinions.

Chapter 8 | Who's on TV?

CHAPTER GOALS

- Learn about themes and stereotyping in television entertainment and the concept of media literacy
- Learn a Listening Strategy: Recognize non-verbal signals that indicate when information is important
- Learn a Note-taking Strategy: Annotate your lecture notes
- Learn a Discussion Strategy: Keep the discussion focused on the topic

Build Background Knowledge

Think about the topic

1. Look at this picture of the cast of a TV show. Then discuss the questions below in pairs.

1. What type of TV show do you think these actors are on? Why do you think so? Is this a type of show that you enjoy? Why or why not?

2. Why do people like to watch TV? What do TV programs offer them?

2. Read this passage from a book about common themes used in television programs in the U.S.

THEMES IN TELEVISION ENTERTAINMENT

Television gives viewers a wide range of entertainment choices. Or does it? When we look at the broad pattern of characters and plots, we can see that most television entertainment in the U.S. includes the same few favorite themes and messages. These can be summarized as follows:

Money. In the TV world, people usually have a lot of nice things: houses, cars, clothes. This sends a message that having a lot of nice things is normal and desirable. In advertising, we **take** this message **for granted**. Advertisers want to attract buyers to their product. Television programs are now delivering a similar message for similar reasons: They want to attract viewers to their shows. We see this in the number of programs featuring rich, beautiful **characters** living in homes and driving cars that a real person in their situation could not possibly afford.

Danger. The world, according to television, is a risky and dangerous place. Television programs like police **dramas** show us a tremendous amount of violence and crime.

Respect. In TV life, people with professional jobs get more respect than people with service or manual jobs, such as waitresses or factory workers. This is true in all kinds of programs, especially **comedy** shows.

Business. Businesspeople cannot be trusted, at least not on TV. In program after program, businesspeople cheat, lie, or use other people.

Fantasy. TV programs reflect a strong desire in viewers for **fantasy**. People like to forget **reality** for an hour and imagine worlds that do not exist, life on other planets, and life after death. Even shows that are not fantasy often try to include some piece of fantasy because they know it will attract viewers. An interesting **aspect** of fantasy programs is the way that they use people's natural fear of the unknown. Things that people cannot explain are usually presented as bad, dangerous, or evil.

Self-interest. People in the television world are extraordinarily interested in themselves. Many characters on TV think only about getting what they want. They are not **conscious** of other people's desires or needs. For example, one man tricks another man in order to win his girlfriend. He doesn't consider the other man's feelings at all, or the girlfriend's. He wants that woman, so he does anything to get her.

These common themes from television are seldom true in real life and usually involve **stereotypes** of people: the lazy janitor, the lying businessperson, the troubled teenager. These stereotypes can be funny, but they can also be insulting and untrue.

3. Fill in the chart with examples or supporting points from the reading on page 79. Then discuss your answers with a partner.

Common Theme on Television		Examples or Details
1.	Having a lot of nice things.	Many programs with rich people/people living in homes/driving cars they can't pay for
2.	The world is dangerous.	
3.	Professional people deserve more respect than workers.	
4.	Businesspeople are not honest.	
5.	People have a strong desire for fantasy.	
6.	People are only interested in themselves.	

4. Circle the answer that correctly completes the definition of the word. Look back at the article on page 79 to check your answers.

1. <u>Characters</u> are the _____ in a book, movie, or television show.
   a. people   **b.** locations
2. <u>Dramas</u> are movies or television programs that are _____.
   a. funny   **b.** serious
3. A <u>comedy</u> is a _____ kind of television program or movie.
   a. serious   **b.** funny
4. <u>Fantasy</u> is a situation that is _____.
   a. true   **b.** from the imagination
5. <u>Reality</u> is the way _____ really is.
   a. television   **b.** life
6. An <u>aspect</u> is one _____ of an idea, situation, or problem.
   a. part   **b.** example
7. To be <u>conscious</u> of something means to be _____ of something.
   a. a part   **b.** aware
8. A <u>stereotype</u> is a _____ idea or image about people or things, which is often untrue.
   a. common   **b.** strange

5. Complete the sentence by choosing a phrase with a similar meaning to the underlined idiom.

Viewers <u>take for granted</u> that people in TV ads are not like real people.
a. accept without thinking about it   **c.** don't understand
b. prefer without really caring

6. Discuss these questions in a small group. Share your answers with the class.

1. Do you agree with the writer that people watch television to forget about the reality of their lives? If you agree, is this a good thing or a bad thing? If you disagree, explain why you think people watch television.

2. Many of the ideas in the article talk about how television does not represent reality well. Do you think this is true? How do you feel about this?

7. With a partner, write down three things in your notebook that you have learned so far about themes in television.

Prepare to Listen and Take Notes

1. To help you understand the listening strategy, discuss the situation below and answer the question.

Imagine you are listening to a lecture and the professor stops talking and writes a word on the board. What should you do?
a. Use this free time to review your notes.
b. Write the word down because it is probably important.

Recognize Non-Verbal Signals for Important Information
In addition to using words to tell you that a piece of information is important, professors use non-verbal signals—gestures and movement—to signal that something is important.
Watch for non-verbal signals about the importance of a point or idea and write the information down.

2. Read the list of non-verbal signals for indicating that something is important. Can you think of others? Discuss them with a partner.

The professor writes down a piece of information
The professor presents the information on a prepared slide
The professor uses gestures: emphasizes an action or an idea with his/her hands, pounds on the podium or table, counts out points on his/her fingers.
The professor leans far forward or moves toward the students
The professor pauses and looks at all the students

Recognize non-verbal signals

3. **Look at the photos of a professor giving a lecture. Then read the three quotes from the lecture. Match the non-verbal signal with the idea the professor is talking about.**

The professor says:

1.    2.    3.

___ **a.** "We'll be discussing at least three common stereotypes in television programming."

___ **b.** "Images of powerful men doing powerful jobs are in **every single program** on TV."

___ **c.** "The selection of TV programs seems extremely wide to average watchers, but not to the experts."

Listen

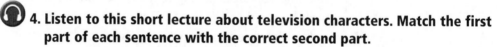 4. **Listen to this short lecture about television characters. Match the first part of each sentence with the correct second part.**

___ **1.** Almost all characters on TV   **a.** get hurt or injured.

___ **2.** TV characters rarely   **b.** are healthy.

___ **3.** Very few TV characters   **c.** are fat or unhealthy.

Follow the lecture

5. **Now follow the short lecture. As you watch, write down four of the non-verbal signals that the speaker uses to indicate important ideas. Then watch once more and write down the important idea.**

1. Non-verbal importance signal: _____

    Important idea: _____

2. Non-verbal importance signal: _____

    Important idea: _____

3. Non-verbal importance signal: _____

    Important idea: _____

4. Non-verbal importance signal: _____

    Important idea: _____

Annotate Your Notes During a Lecture

Professors present a lot of information in one lecture, and you might not understand everything they say. It's important to write down the questions or difficulties you have in your notes and refer to these after the lecture.

Annotate your notes with questions or reminders to yourself of something you need to study after the lecture.

Annotate your notes

6. Look at one student's notes on the short lecture about television characters from Exercises 4 and 5. Notice how she has annotated her notes (in bold). List the types of annotation she uses.

> TV Themes
>
> Health of chars on TV=useful for understanding power of TV media **(look up "media")**
>
>   Almost all TV characters = healthy
>
>   even w/ shooting/car crash **(???)**
>
>   Rarely get hurt
>
>   even w/o seat belts
>
>   **(Re-read textbk chap. on this)**
>
>   Eating=unhealthy
>
>   Too much food, candy, coffee
>
>   * Very few fat/unhealthy people **Why is this possible?**

Types of annotation

_____

_____

_____

_____

_____

_____

Listen and Take Notes

Make predictions

▷ p. 8

1. Before the lecture, think about everything you have learned and discussed on the topic of themes on television. What do you expect to learn more about in the lecture? Write three predictions below. Compare your predictions with a partner.

1. _____

2. _____

3. _____

Follow the lecture

▷ annotation, p. 83

2. Now follow the lecture and take notes using annotation. Remember to pay attention to non-verbal signals for important information.

3. How well were you able to recognize the lecture language? Check the statement that best describes you. Explain your answer.

I was able to understand when an idea was important
— all the time   — some of the time   — almost never

4. Use your notes to answer these questions.

1. What are the three ways that the characters on TV are different from people in the real world?

_____

_____

_____

2. What are some of the television stereotypes of men? Describe them.

_____

_____

_____

3. What is one television stereotype of women? Describe it.

_____

_____

_____

4. What are some concerns about the way TV presents the world and people?

_____

_____

_____

Assess your notes

 p. 9

5. Were you able to answer the questions in Exercise 4 using the information in your notes? Compare your notes with a few other students. Discuss the differences and help each other fill in any missing information. Complete your notes.

Summarize the lecture

 p. 19

6. Work with a partner and take turns. Review your notes from the lecture. Then explain the main points of the lecture to your partner. Talk for 2-3 minutes only.

Discuss the Issues

Discussion Strategy

Keep the Discussion Focused
During a discussion, students sometimes bring up ideas that are not closely related to the topic. In this situation, the other students should politely try to bring the discussion back to the original topic. Use expressions to keep the discussion focused.

Keep the discussion focused

1. Read the expressions for keeping a discussion focused. Can you add others to the list?

I think we're getting off the topic/subject.
Could we go back to _____ ?
I think we're getting off track.
Maybe we should get back to the question.
Let's get back on track.
Maybe we could talk about that later.
Let's stay focused.
That's a good point, but for now let's stay with . . .

_____

_____

_____

Practice keeping the discussion focused

2. In groups of four, read the questions and discuss them. Keep the conversation going until every student has had a chance to practice using the language for keeping the discussion focused. Use your own ideas or the ones given below.

1. When do you watch TV?
   Possible Ideas

Right after waking up	During meals
Before going to bed	When there is nothing to do
After work	When there is an important event

2. What do you like and dislike about television?
   Possible Ideas

Like	**Dislike**
TV is a no-brainer	TV has too many ads
It's fun to look at beautiful people	It has too many stupid characters
It's a good way to learn languages	It hurts my eyes

Discuss the ideas in the lecture

3. Discuss these ideas from the lecture with your classmates. Remember to use the phrases for keeping the discussion focused.

1. In your opinion, how do television programs show viewers a world that is different from reality? How do you feel about this?

2. How important is media literacy? Do you think it can really affect people's TV viewing habits and preferences? Why or why not?

3. If you could give advice to television writers on how to create a show that you and your friends would like, what would you suggest? What type of show would it be? What kinds of characters would it have? Why would people watch this show?

4. Look back at your notes. What was another idea in the lecture that you found important and interesting? Tell the class why you think it is important or interesting and ask for their opinions

Unit Wrap-Up

1. **Work in small groups. Create a survey on news habits. Find out your subjects' ages and then ask information about the way they get their news. Then create charts that show the differences in news habits by age. Present and explain your charts to the class.**

   - age group: 15-20, 21-25, 26-30, 30-35, over 35

   - how often people of different ages get the news

   - the percentage of news that they get from TV, print media, and the Internet

2. **The lecture compares the number and percentages of the men and women, rich people, and professional people that are on TV to the number and percentages that exist in real life. Conduct a survey outside of class to see how closely people guess the numbers in each of the categories. How great is the difference? What accounts for the difference? Discuss your results with the class.**

3. **Work in small groups. Cut out a major news story from your local paper. Print out a story on the same topic from an Internet Web site. Compare the two stories and answer the questions. Share your answers with the class.**

   1. Does the issue seem equally serious and important in both articles? If not, which medium makes the issue seem more important? What are some reasons for this?

   2. Which article is written better? Why do you think so?

   3. Which article do you think covers the story better? Why?

   Notes: _____

   _____

   _____

   _____

   _____

   _____

   _____

   _____

unit 5

LINGUISTICS

linguistics \lɪŋˈgwɪstɪks\ The scientific study
of language

What's Up with Slang

- Learn about the origins and use of slang in English
- Learn a Listening Strategy: Recognize changes in pronunciation that signal when information is important
- Learn a Note-taking Strategy: Edit your notes
- Learn a Discussion Strategy: Encourage other students to participate during a discussion

Build Background Knowledge

Think about the topic

1. Look at the cartoon. Then discuss the questions below in pairs.

"Is everything all right, Jeffrey? You never call me 'dude' anymore."

1. Why do people use slang? Is slang necessary? Why or why not?
2. Does every language have slang? Give some examples of slang in other languages, if you can.

2. Read this Web site article about the purposes and value of slang in society.

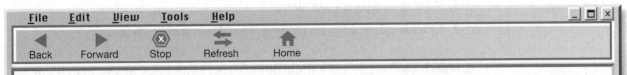

File   Edit   View   Tools   Help

◄ Back   ► Forward   ⊗ Stop   ⇄ Refresh   🏠 Home

Get Your Own Slang!

I'm standing outside Swenson's Internet Café in Kansas City, Missouri, and a group of teenagers is talking:

Teenager 1:	Yo, dawg, wuz crackin'?
Teenager 2:	Chillaxin' in my crib. You, Hom's?
Teenager 1:	Got mad stuff to do.
Teenager 2:	A-ight. Peace out.

I'm only ten years older than those kids, but I need one of them to translate for me. I've just entered a new culture, and all the rules, at least for language, are different here. The conversation seems **casual**, but I don't even know if they're being nice to each other or saying something **offensive**.

There's a new term for today's teenagers: The Millennial Generation. But you won't find such a formal phrase in the average teenager's vocabulary. What do they call each other? "Dude," "Homey," or some other **informal** and sometimes strange **expression** to show that they belong to the same group.

Despite the way they look and speak, I think that today's teenagers are no different from any other generation. Teenagers have always used slang to identify with others in their age group and to show their independence from adults at the same time. Using slang gives their "club" its own language. When teenagers use slang, they're communicating their connection with each other, their group **identity**. These kids aren't just talking about what they're doing—they're connecting with each other by speaking the same language to talk about something that is probably only **relevant** to them.

Like teenagers of every generation, today's teenagers have many ways to establish their independent identity. They wear the same sorts of **popular** styles in clothing. Friends and larger **peer** groups travel in packs, listen to the same music, and all do the same activities. And yes, they speak whatever slang is currently **in style**.

Let the teenagers have their slang. We had ours, so it's fair. Being part of a group is important and "secret" languages are fun. The next time you hear teenagers speaking what sounds like a foreign language, just smile and say to yourself, "Cool."

3. Answer the questions about the article on page 91. Then discuss your answers with a partner.

   1. Why do teenagers use slang?

   2. In what other ways do teenagers establish their own identity?

4. Match the words with their definitions. Look back at the article on page 91 to check your answers.

   ____ **1.** casual   **a.** connected or related

   ____ **2.** offensive   **b.** a person of the same age or in the same type of job

   ____ **3.** informal   **c.** relaxed and friendly

   ____ **4.** expression   **d.** the qualities of a group that make it different from others

   ____ **5.** identity   **e.** unpleasant or insulting

   ____ **6.** relevant   **f.** a group of words that go together

   ____ **7.** popular   **g.** the opposite of formal

5. Circle the phrase with a similar meaning to the underlined idiom.

In the 1950s, most men had short hair. In the 1960s, long hair was <u>in style</u>.
a. attractive to the opposite sex   **c.** fashionable at a particular time
b. unusual and unpopular

6. Discuss these questions in a small group. Share your answers with the class.

   1. Are teenagers the only peer group that uses slang? What other groups might have their own slang?

   2. Is slang a good way for a group to establish its identity? Why or why not?

7. With a partner, write down three things in your notebook that you have learned so far about slang.

Prepare to Listen and Take Notes

1. To help you understand the listening strategy, discuss the situation below and answer the question.

Imagine you are listening to a lecture. As she is making a point, the professor speaks louder. What does this mean?

a. The professor is angry with the students and wants them to leave.

b. This point is important and the students should notice it.

Listening Strategy

Recognize Changes in Pronunciation

Professors often change the tone of their voice or their pronunciation to emphasize or clarify a word or idea. Recognizing these signals can help you catch important points more effectively.

Listen for pronunciation signals that professors use to clarify or emphasize a word or idea.

Pronunciation signals

2. Read the list of pronunciation signals. Can you add others to the list?

Pronunciation Signals to Emphasize One Word

Professors say the word

- more loudly

- more slowly

- with higher intonation

Pronunciation Signals to Emphasize a Group of Words

Professors

- slow down as they say an important group of words.

- pause before saying an important group of words.

- pronounce each word separately or give each word special emphasis

_____

_____

_____

Recognize pronunciation signals

3. Listen to this short lecture about teenagers and slang. Match the first part of each sentence with the correct second part.

_____ **1.** Teenagers today   **a.** worry about teenagers' slang.

_____ **2.** Parents of teenagers   **b.** have fun with the language.

_____ **3.** Slang is a way to   **c.** have creative and interesting slang.

4. **Listen to the lecture again. As you listen, write down the important word or words. Then listen once more and write down the pronunciation signal that you heard.**

Use these abbreviations:

L   for louder
S   for slower
H   for higher intonation
P   for a pause

1. Word or group of words _____

_____

Pronunciation signal _____

2. Word or group of words _____

_____

Pronunciation signal _____

3. Word or group of words _____

_____

Pronunciation signal _____

4. Word or group of words _____

_____

Pronunciation signal _____

5. Word or group of words _____

_____

Pronunciation signal _____

6. Word or group of words _____

_____

Pronunciation signal _____

Edit Your Notes
During a lecture, students take notes very quickly. It's possible to miss something, write something incompletely, or write something down incorrectly. After the lecture, read through your notes quickly and edit them while the lecture is still fresh in your mind.

Edit your notes

5. Look at one student's notes from the short lecture on teenagers and slang in Exercise 4. Then list the ways that she edited her notes below.

> a lot of   andard
> ↑ Today's teenagers use ↑ slang + speak st / Engl.
> teens use slang—then switch to ~~more~~ **in**formal English
> Switch again + use all kinds of technical **language**
>   Ex: **talk about computers**
>   **something they have studied**
> They know when to use slang + **when not to use it**

_____

_____

_____

6. Read the transcript from the short lecture on teenagers and slang in Exercise 4. Then look at one student's notes and edit the notes to make them more complete.

Now, some parents of teenagers worry when they hear their children use slang. They worry that their language is too informal or that other people won't understand them. They are also afraid that other people will think that their kids don't know how to speak English properly. We hear this all the time.

> Parents worry when they hear slang.
>   Language is too formal
>   Other people won't understand them
>   They don't know how to speak English

Listen and Take Notes

Make predictions

1. Before the lecture, think about everything you have learned and discussed on the topic of slang. What do you expect to learn more about in the lecture? Write three predictions below. Compare your predictions with a partner.

   1. _____

   2. _____

   3. _____

Follow the lecture

2. Now follow the lecture and take notes. Remember to listen for the pronunciation signals used to clarify or emphasize a word or idea.

Chapter 9 What's Up with Slang

3. How well were you able to recognize the lecture language? Check the statement that best describes you. Explain your answer.

I was able to hear when a word or words was being emphasized or clarified
— most of the time   — some of the time   — almost never

4. Use your notes to answer these questions.

1. Use your own words to explain the meaning of slang.

_____

_____

_____

2. What are the reasons people use slang?

_____

_____

_____

3. What are the three ways that slang is created? Explain each way.

_____

_____

_____

4. Why is slang controversial?

_____

_____

_____

Edit your notes

 p. 95

5. Quickly re-read your notes and look for any information that is missing, incorrect, or incomplete. Edit your notes while the lecture is still fresh in your mind.

Summarize the lecture

 p. 19

6. Work with a partner and take turns. Review your notes from the lecture. Then explain the main points of the lecture to your partner. Talk for 2-3 minutes only.

Discuss the Issues

Discussion Strategy

Encourage Other Students to Participate in a Discussion
To create an interesting, thorough, and lively discussion, everyone in the group must contribute his or her ideas. But speaking isn't easy for everyone. You can help create a better discussion by asking other students to offer their ideas. Use expressions to politely encourage other students to participate in the discussion.

Encourage others to participate

1. Read the expressions for encouraging other students to participate. Can you add others to the list?

What does everyone else think?
Has everyone shared their ideas?
Lee, what do you think?
Lee, can you add something here?
Lee, how do you see the situation?
What do you think, Lee?
How about you, Lee? What do you think?
We haven't heard from Lee yet.
Let's hear from some others in the group.

_____

_____

_____

2. In groups of four, read the questions and discuss them. Keep the conversation going until every student has had a chance to practice encouraging other students to contribute to the discussion. Use your own ideas or the ones below.

  1. What are some of your favorite slang expressions?

  2. Should people use slang?

   Possible Ideas

Yes	No
It helps express ideas better	It's not correct language
People can connect with each other	People don't understand it
Can be secret from other people	It excludes people

3. Discuss these ideas from the lecture with your classmates. Remember to use the phrases for encouraging other students to participate.

  1. What are the advantages and disadvantages of using slang for these different groups in the United States?

   • friends

   • older people

   • ethnic groups

   • co-workers or people in the same line of work

   • people living in the same region

  2. Does it matter that slang sometimes breaks the rules of language? Why or why not?

  3. Imagine a world in which slang did not exist. What would this world be like? For example, would teenagers and adults get along better because they always used the same language? Would people be more honest? Would you like to live in this world? Why or why not?

  4. Look back at your notes. What was another idea in the lecture that you found important and interesting? Tell the class why you think it is important or interesting and ask for their opinions.

CHAPTER GOALS

- Learn about people's attitudes toward English around the world
- Review and practice all listening strategies
- Review and practice all note-taking strategies
- Learn a Discussion Strategy: Bring a group to a consensus during a discussion

Build Background Knowledge

Think about the topic

1. Look at the picture. Then discuss the questions below in pairs.

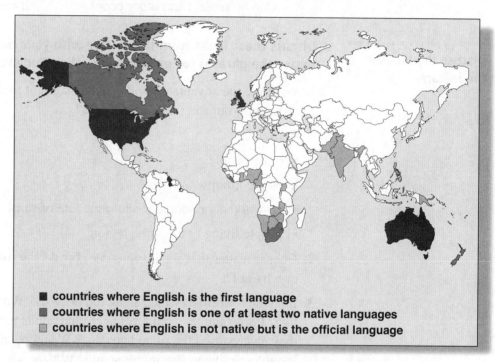

- ■ countries where English is the first language
- ■ countries where English is one of at least two native languages
- ■ countries where English is not native but is the official language

1. How many people in the world do you think speak English as a first language? As a second language? Give reasons for your guesses.

2. Think of the people that you know who speak English as a second language. Why do/did they want or need to learn English?

2. Read this article about how English is used in international business and politics.

International English

There is a **worldwide** trend toward international business—businesses in different countries coming together to trade goods and services. The United States, Canada, and Mexico have all signed the North American Free Trade Agreement (NAFTA). This is an international agreement to lower **economic barriers** between the countries and end many limits on the buying and selling of goods.

Another example of this worldwide trend is the European Union (EU). The EU is an organization through which many countries in Europe have united economically and **politically**. The 500 million people living in the European Union share common institutions and official policy agreements. These agreements make it easier for the **members** to do business together.

There are **significant benefits** for the countries involved in these agreements. The European Union, for example, has a much more powerful economy than that of the individual countries. In fact, the EU and the United States are the two largest economies in the world. Together they make up about half of the entire world's economy.

International agreements such as NAFTA and the EU promote economic and political unity between countries. This means that member nations have to make decisions together about policies in many areas: agriculture, consumer affairs, business competition, the environment, energy, transport, and trade. Language **plays a role**—an important role—in policy meetings. For example, when the EU comes together to make decisions, many translators are needed. These translators keep Europe working smoothly in at least 20 different languages. On May 1, 2004, ten new countries joined the EU, bringing the total number of member nations to twenty-five. The number of possible combinations of languages in any interaction within the EU increased to nearly 400.

With so many different languages, everyday conversations increasingly require a language that most of the people can already speak **fluently**—such as English. Most people in Brussels, the headquarters for the EU, speak at least two or three languages, so English is increasingly the common language in any gathering of more than a few people. This situation is not **unique**. English is also used in many NAFTA meetings and other international gatherings around the world. The increased need for English in political circles will only add to a trend that has existed for years: using English for day-to-day business exchanges.

As more and more countries come together for political or business purposes, the need for a common language will only increase. Based on current trends, English seems to be the obvious choice.

———————◆———————

3. Answer the questions about the article on page 101. Then discuss your answers with a partner.

1. What are two examples of the trend toward international business?

2. What is a benefit of countries making international agreements?

3. Why is English being used in EU meetings more and more often?

4. Circle the answer that correctly completes the definition of the word. Look back at the article on page 101 to check your answers.

1. Something that is <u>worldwide</u> is _____ in the world.
   a. everywhere   **b.** in a few places

2. <u>Economic barriers</u> are _____ that prevent countries from doing business together.
   a. rules about language   **b.** rules about money

3. Something that is <u>political</u> has to do with the _____ of a country.
   a. language   **b.** government

4. A <u>member</u> of an organization is a _____ that belongs to a bigger group.
   a. individual person or group   **b.** set of rules

5. When something is <u>significant</u>, it has an _____ effect or influence.
   a. important   **b.** unimportant

6. A <u>benefit</u> is the _____ that you get from something.
   a. problem   **b.** advantage

7. To be <u>fluent</u> in a language means that you can speak it _____.
   a. at a high level   **b.** at a low level

8. When something is <u>unique</u>, it is _____.
   a. different and special   **b.** typical and good

5. Circle the phrase with a similar meaning to the underlined idiom.

Language, politics, and culture all <u>play a role</u> in international agreements.
a. are involved   **b.** are not present

6. Discuss these questions in a small group. Share your answers with the class.

1. Why do international organizations like to have a common language?

2. Why do you think English is often the language chosen?

7. With a partner, write down three things in your notebook that you have learned so far about the use of English in international organizations.

 p. 5

Prepare to Listen and Take Notes

1. To help you understand the listening strategy, discuss the situation below and answer the question.

Imagine that you are in a college class getting ready to listen to a two-hour lecture. Make a list of the listening strategies that you

feel confident in: _____

need to work on: _____

find the most helpful: _____

Listening Strategy	**Listening Strategy Review** Review all the listening strategies that you have learned in this book.

Review listening strategies

2. Look back at the strategies that have been presented in this book. Review them by giving some examples of lecture language for each one.

▷ p. 5

1. Listen for the topic of a lecture _____

_____

▷ p. 5, 15

2. Listen for the big picture of a lecture _____

_____

▷ p. 27

3. Listen for transitions in a lecture _____

_____

▷ p. 37

4. Listen for definitions in a lecture _____

_____

▷ p. 49

5. Listen for examples in a lecture _____

_____

▷ p. 59

6. Listen for explanations in a lecture _____

_____

▷ p. 71

7. Listen for important information in a lecture _____

_____

3. Listen to this short lecture on the business of teaching English worldwide. Match the first part of each sentence with the correct second part.

_____ 1. English is taught in   **a.** trained and untrained teachers.

_____ 2. English is taught by   **b.** English speaking countries.

_____ 3. Ideally, English is learned in   **c.** schools, businesses, and governments.

4. Listen to the lecture again. As you listen, write down the lecture language. Then listen once more and write down the information that follows each instance of lecture language.

1. Topic lecture language: _____

    Topic: _____

2. Big picture lecture language: _____

_____

3. Transition lecture language: _____

    New idea: _____

4. Definition lecture language: _____

    Definition: _____

5. Example lecture language: _____

    Example: _____

6. Explanation lecture language: _____

    Explanation: _____

7. Importance lecture language: _____

    Important information: _____

Note-Taking Strategy Review
Review all the note-taking strategies that you have learned in this book.

Review note-taking strategies

5. **Read the transcript from a lecture on the trend toward the use of English in international business. Then, look at one student's notes from the lecture. Identify which seven note-taking strategies the student has used and write them in your notebook. Give at least one example for each strategy.**

....

I'd like to focus today on how decisions get made between members of trade groups like the North American Free Trade Agreement, which is referred to as NAFTA, and the European Union, which is commonly referred to as the EU. All the member nations of trade groups like NAFTA and the EU have to make decisions together about a variety of policies. They have to agree on policies that affect things like agriculture, consumer affairs, business competition, the environment, energy, transport, and trade. You get the picture? All these decisions get made in policy meetings.

Language plays a role—an important role—in all these policy meetings. Let me give you an example of what I mean by the importance of language. On May 1, 2004, ten new countries joined the EU. At this point the number of member nations is 25—that is 25 different countries with almost the same number of languages. So, you can imagine that when the EU gets together to make decisions, a large number of translators are needed. These translators keep these policy discussions happening by offering translation into at least 20 different languages. So, that is what happens at official meetings in Brussels, the headquarters of the European Union.

....

```
        Decision making for trade groups
  →       ex. North Am. Free Trade Agreement (NAFTA)
  ◯         European Union (EU)
        Policy meetings:
          make decisions about:
            agriculture
            consumer affairs
            business competition
            environment + policy energy
            transportation + trade
        * Language plays imp. role @ policy meetings
            # of countries @ meetings in 2004 = 25
            # of diff languages - 20 languages for translation
                    ----check what these are
```

Listen and Take Notes

Make predictions

▷ p. 8

1. **Before the lecture, think about everything you have learned and discussed on the topic of global English. What do you expect to learn more about in the lecture? Write three predictions below. Compare your predictions with a partner.**

1. _____

2. _____

3. _____

Follow the lecture

2. **Now follow the lecture and take notes. Remember to listen for all the lecture language that you have learned.**

3. How well did you recognize the lecture language? Check the statement that best describes you. Explain your answer.

___ I was able to recognize most of the lecture language.

___ I was able to recognize some of the lecture language.

4. Use your notes to answer these questions.

1. How many native speakers of English are there in the world? How many people speak some English?

_____

_____

_____

2. What two trends have an influence on the growing use of English globally?

_____

_____

_____

3. What are the four points of view about the spread of English presented in the lecture? Explain them.

_____

_____

_____

4. Some people fear the worldwide spread of English. What are two things that they fear might happen?

_____

_____

_____

5. Were you able to answer the questions in Exercise 4 using the information in your notes? Compare your notes with a few other students. Discuss the differences and help each other fill in any missing information. Complete your notes.

6. Work with a partner and take turns. Review your notes from the lecture. Then explain the main points of the lecture to your partner. Talk for 2-3 minutes only.

Discuss the Issues

Discussion Strategy

Bring the Group to a Consensus
A consensus is an agreement among a group of people. Student study groups sometimes have to come to a consensus on one point of view or idea and present it to the whole class. To do this, the members of the group need to compare ideas, discuss them, then choose or compromise on one. Use expressions to help bring the group to a consensus.

**Bring the group
to a consensus**

1. Read the expressions for coming to a consensus in a discussion. Can you add others to the list?

Does everyone agree?
So, is everyone satisfied with this?
Does anyone have anything to add?
Let's take a vote. Raise your hand if you agree with this idea.
We're going to have to compromise. Maria, how strongly do
    you feel about _____?
What can we all live with?

_____

_____

_____

Practice coming to a consensus

2. In groups of four, read the questions and discuss them. Keep the conversation going until every student has had a chance to practice coming to a consensus. Use your own ideas or the ones below.

1. What are the three best ways to learn English?
   Possible ideas

   watch TV   take a grammar class

   make friends with native speakers   read in English

2. Why is it important to learn English? Give the three top reasons.
   Possible ideas

   to listen to pop music   to earn more money

   to get a job   to use the Internet

Discuss the ideas in the lecture

3. Discuss these ideas from the lecture with your classmates. Remember to use the phrases for coming to a consensus.

1. Which of the four opinions about the spread of English do you agree with? Why?

2. In the lecture, the professor says that the main language used on the Internet is English. When you use the Internet, do you only visit English language websites or do you visit websites that use other languages? Explain your answer.

3. Imagine there is a group of businesses that would like to make a trade agreement. Many languages are represented in the group: Mandarin, Spanish, English, Arabic. The group will do business equally in all regions. Is a common language necessary? If so, which language? If not, describe how multiple languages could work.

4. Look back at your notes. What was another idea in the lecture that you found important and interesting? Tell the class why you think it is important or interesting and ask for their opinions.

Unit Wrap-Up

1. Should English teachers teach slang to their students? As a class, brainstorm the pros and cons of this issue. Then divide the class into two parts and debate the pros and cons.

2. Interview at least three people from a non-English speaking country. Find out their opinion about the spread and use of English in their home country. How do their opinions compare with the opinions discussed in the lecture? Discuss your ideas with your classmates.

3. There are many Web sites that present the slang used by different groups of people. Go online and find three categories of slang that are new to you. For each type of slang, write down the group that uses the slang and three good examples of it. Make sure the slang is appropriate to a school environment.

Notes: _____

_____

_____

_____

_____

_____

_____

_____

_____

_____

_____

_____

Teacher's Notes

Organization of the Book

Lecture Ready 2: Strategies for Academic Listening, Note-taking, and Discussion contains five units with two chapters in each unit. Each unit focuses on one field of academic study. Each chapter is built around a lecture from a typical course within the field. In each chapter, students are presented with and practice listening, note-taking, and discussion strategies.

Chapter Guide

Strategy Boxes

Throughout the book, strategies are presented and explained in strategy boxes. These boxes are tabbed within each chapter for easy navigation. After a strategy is introduced, it is recycled in subsequent chapters. At each instance of recycling, a page number tab in the left margin directs students to the original strategy box for quick reference.

Build Background Knowledge

The purpose of this part of the chapter is to introduce the topic and help students think about what they already know so that they can be more active listeners during the lecture.

Think about the topic

In this section, students activate current knowledge of the chapter topic and begin to build understanding and topic vocabulary. Students look at a visual prompt and answer questions about it in order to share information. Encourage broad discussion— there are no right or wrong answers.

Read

The readings employ common academic formats and are based on information from authentic sources. They introduce information that is relevant to the topic of the lecture but not the main ideas of the lecture. The readings also present some of the key vocabulary from the lecture in context. Students should read for general comprehension.

Check your comprehension

This aims to reinforce students' comprehension of the larger ideas in the reading. Again, the goal is to help them build background knowledge about the ideas in the coming lecture.

Expand your vocabulary

Words and phrases from the reading that will be used in the lecture are addressed here. These words and phrases are important for understanding the key ideas in the lecture. In most cases, they come from the **Academic Word List**, so learning them will be valuable for future academic pursuits as well.

Discuss the reading

This continues to build background knowledge and add to what they know about the topic. These questions are designed to get students to react with opinions and personal experiences related to the ideas in the readings. Students do not need to reference the reading; instead, an open-ended discussion should be encouraged.

Review what you know

This is a strategy that good listeners employ automatically: They consciously think about what they know in preparation for taking in new information. Rather than having students begin listening right after they build background knowledge, students are directed to take a moment to collect their background knowledge. They will revisit this section before they watch the lecture.

Prepare to Listen and Take Notes

This part has two purposes: to present the targeted lecture language for that chapter and to present note-taking strategies.

Lecture Language: Students learn about and practice the strategy of recognizing lecture language—the specific expressions that professors use to guide students through the ideas in the lecture. This language, which can be found in lectures from all disciplines, ranges from expressions that signal the topic of a lecture to non-verbal expressions that signal when a piece of information is important.

Note-taking Strategy: Students learn about and practice a specific note-taking strategy. These strategies range from using a simple outline form to describing visuals in your notes.

Prepare to Listen and Take Notes starts with an activity that introduces the chapter listening strategy in a friendly way. Thinking about the situation helps students discover the need for learning the listening strategy featured in the chapter. Give students time to discuss the situation with a partner before they share with the class.

Listening strategy

Have students read the Listening Strategy box. Then have students work with the set of lecture language expressions. You can have students read the expressions and add others to the list. Or you can first elicit the expressions that students already know then look at the list to confirm what they know and add others.

Students practice recognizing the chapter's lecture language in a printed excerpt before listening to the practice lecture. You may prefer to work with the excerpt as a class, using an overhead transparency.

Listen for lecture language

Students listen to a short practice lecture related to the centerpiece lecture. This practice lecture uses simplified content so that students can focus on listening for the target lecture language.

Students listen first for content, in order to understand the ideas. After this activity, have students share their answers with the class to gain confidence.

Students then listen a second time in order to focus on recognizing the chapter lecture language. Since the listening focus is so specific, you might need to replay the practice lecture in order for student to catch all the instances asked for. First, have students listen and write down only the target lecture language. Then have them listen again and write down the information referenced by the target lecture language.

Note-taking strategy

Have students study the Note-taking Strategy box. In chapters 3 and 4, students learn a body of note-taking symbols and abbreviations. In other chapters, students analyze the note-taking strategy by examining an example of student notes that employ the strategy. You might want to show these sample notes on a transparency and point out the specific features of the note-taking strategy.

Students then practice the note-taking strategy by reading an excerpt from a lecture and taking notes on it. Have students compare their notes in pairs.

Listen and Take Notes

In this part, students put their new strategies to work by watching an actual lecture and taking notes on it.

Make predictions

The section begins with a prediction activity. The purpose of this exercise is to remind students of their earlier topic work and help them prepare to take in new information.

Follow the lecture

Students are now ready to "attend" the lecture. In Chapters 1–6, a note-taking outline has been provided to guide students toward the key ideas in the lecture. These outlines help them focus their listening and provide a structure for their notes. This scaffolding decreases as the book progresses so that by Chapter 7 students are taking notes unaided.

Assess your comprehension

After the lecture, students assess three key components: their comprehension of lecture language, their general understanding of some of the key points in the lecture, and their notes.

First, they evaluate their own understanding of the lecture language and tie their comprehension of the lecture to their ability to follow the lecture language.

Students then answer basic comprehension questions about the larger ideas in the lecture using their notes. Encourage students to share their answers and also to explain how they arrived at their answer—to explain what the lecturer actually said.

Next, students assess their notes to see what information they might have missed or misunderstood. Encourage students to discuss the differences in their respective notes and try to understand why they missed or mistook something.

Summarize the lecture

Here, students summarize the lecture to consolidate what they have learned and find out how well they have understood the important ideas in the lecture. The goal is to enhance comprehension of important ideas in the lecture by putting them in their own words. Summarizing the lecture aloud with a partner gives students training in an authentic academic activity—comparing and discussing notes with a classmate. Summarizing is an important strategy that will be useful throughout their academic careers.

Explain to the students that, if they find they have too little to say, this is a good sign that they missed

information and should look back at their notes. Encourage students to use the summary language presented in Chapter 2. Point out that they do not need a partner to summarize. This is an excellent strategy to use on their own.

Discuss the Issues

This part is aimed at providing students with appropriate words and phrases for classroom or small-group discussion of the ideas in a lecture. In doing so, these strategies also inform students about the basic expectations for participation and conduct in a discussion setting. Like the listening and note-taking strategies, discussion strategies become progressively more sophisticated, going from "entering a discussion" to "bringing the group to a consensus."

Discussion strategy

Have students read the Discussion Strategy box. Then have students work with the set of discussion expressions. You can have students read the expressions and add others to the list. Or you can first elicit the expressions that students already know then look at the list to confirm what they know and add others.

Discussion practice

In this role-play activity, students are given the chance to practice the discussion language in a more guided way. The content in this section is easily accessible so that the focus can be on practicing the discussion language. Be sure to monitor the groups as they do their role-plays and hold students accountable for their use of the discussion language.

Discuss the ideas in the lecture

Students now bring all their knowledge of the content and the discussion strategy together in a real classroom or small-group discussion of ideas in the lecture. Encourage them to have their lecture notes with them, as they should refer to actual lecture content when appropriate. Encourage students to use the discussion language they have just learned. You may want to appoint a group member to keep track of this.

Unit Wrap-Up

At the end of each unit (so, at the end of every second chapter), there is a Unit Wrap-Up that aims to get students to synthesize the topics in the two chapters and think more conceptually and critically about the broader theme. You can assign these activities or not—they are not strictly part of the units or chapters.

Students get a taste of academic project work such as planning and carrying out a survey, drawing conclusions from survey data, presenting their findings and conclusions before an audience, preparing an argument for or against a topic in a debate, role playing a decision-making situation such as a city council meeting (how should the city spend this money—a or b, and why) or workplace needs-assessment (who would you want on your team and why).

About the Authors

Peg Sarosy

Peg Sarosy is an Academic Coordinator at the American Language Institute at San Francisco State University. She previously taught at San Francisco State University in the ESL department and the Design and Industry department. She taught academic preparation at the University of California - Berkeley intensive English program and was a USIS Teacher Trainer in the Czech Republic. She has a Master's Degree in TESOL from San Francisco State University. Peg is co-author of *Lecture Ready 1* and *Lecture Ready 2*, and a series editor for *Lecture Ready 3*.

Kathy Sherak

Kathy Sherak is Director of the American Language Institute at San Francisco State University. She previously taught in San Francisco State University's ESL program and was a Fulbright Teacher Trainer in Italy. She is the author of the Teacher's Manual for *Grammar Sense Book 3* from Oxford University Press. She has a Master's Degree in TESOL from San Francisco State University. Kathy is co-author of *Lecture Ready 1* and *Lecture Ready 2*, and a series editor for *Lecture Ready 3*.

Notes

Notes

Notes

Notes

Notes